P9-AQB-012

WOMEN OF FAITH

THEIR UNTOLD STORIES REVEALED

Compiled by Rhonda Branch Yearby

Featuring Miss Kay Robertson & 40 Contributing Authors

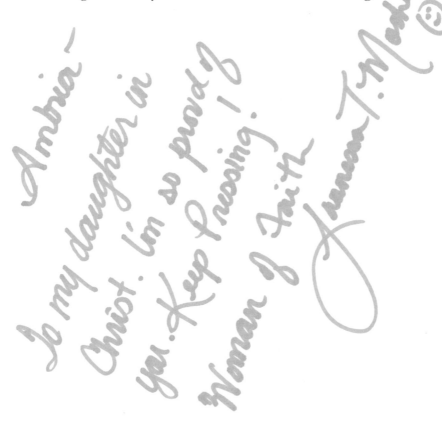

Ambria~

To my daughter in Christ. I'm so proud of you. Keep Pressing!

Woman of Faith

Juanna T. Motley

Women of Faith

Their Untold Stories Revealed

Copyright © 2016 Rhonda Branch Yearby All rights reserved.

ISBN: 9781540863560

BY Publishing

BY Publishing

POB 330

Grambling, Louisiana 71245

All rights reserved. No part of this book may be reproduced in any manner whatsoever, and it may not be stored in a retrieval system, transmitted, or otherwise copied for public or private use, without written permission other than "fair use" as brief quotations embodied in articles and reviews.

Book Cover Design: Elizabeth Williams

Graphics & Promotions: Elizabeth Williams, Stacie Flowers

Senior Editor & Publisher: Rhonda Branch Yearby

Editors: Dormeka Pearce & Teresa Hawley Howard

Interviewers: Dormeka Pearce, Teresa Hawley Howard, Rhonda Branch Yearby

DEDICATION

To my Lord & Saviour Jesus Christ who is the head of my life!

To Miss. Kay Robertson, you stepped out on faith to support me as a Christian sister, friend and mentor! All I can say is you have left me SPEECHLESS and given me UNSPEAKABLE JOY!!I am forever grateful for the LOVE you have shown me!!!! Thank you!

To Dormeka Pearce, Teresa Hawley Howard, Stacie Flowers, & Elizabeth Williams without you Ladies this book would not be possible!!! Thanks for all your hard work and belief in Rhonda Branch Ministries.

As **Women of Faith**, we need to share our testimonies, our pain, our trials and our salvation with the world. God calls us to be a light into the whole world. To be sharers of the Good News. We are to be disciples and go out and bring souls to Christ. How we now use that testimony is to inspire and encourage the next generation.

– Rhonda Branch Yearby

TABLE OF CONTENTS

INTRODUCTION

In this anthology of inspirational stories, told by women from diverse cultures from around the world, you will discover what their faith means to them and how it has helped them to overcome adversity in their lives.

While all are different, these true stories share a common heart... an undeniable and profound faith that has seen them through hardships and helped them overcome remarkable odds and adversity.

May these true stories give you the strength and inspiration to make the changes you need to see in your life, with faith, love and maybe a bit of humor

Women of Faith is a program of Rhonda Branch Ministries which collaborates with BY Publishing and empowers women and girls to become authors. Enjoy your copy of "Women of Faith" today and support these amazing women in their aspirations. It is, above all else, a source of encouragement.

FOREWORD

Our lives are full of up and downs. We will face trying times, times when we feel we cannot go on; it is in these times we must rely on our faith.

"For by grace you have been saved through faith. And this is not your own doing; it is the gift of God." Ephesians 2:8

As a mother, grandmother, mentor and Matriarch of the Robertson family; I want my life and my legacy to make a difference in the world. I want everyone to learn from my experiences, my detours and my mistakes. Yes, we all make them. By sharing our stories, we can help guide the next generation. That is what we have accomplished in this beautiful book. We have shared our hearts, our tests, our trials and our faith with you.

As you read each of the stories ask God to show you the way. Let their stories strengthen your faith, renew your belief and open your heart. Learn to lean on God's understanding and not your own. Let this book bless you and lead you to a closer walk with Jesus.

Remember we are never more than a song of praise a way from God. Call out to him and He will answer. So, leave your cares at God's feet and let Him lead and guide you. May you be blessed and encouraged by the courage of all the women who shared their stories from around the globe.

It is my prayer that our tests, our trials and our testimonies will help to uplift, inspire and save the next generation. The greatest legacy we can leave is to be a woman who shares the gospel. Not only in church, but in every moment of our lives. To bring His word and His salvation to every corner of this world.

One of the key elements in your faith journey is learning to reflect on what you have learned and how you plan to apply it to your daily life. In Rhonda Branch Yearby's new book Women of Faith: Their Untold Stories Revealed, you will learn how writing can enrich and guide your journey in new and exciting ways.

--Miss Kay Robertson Matriarch of A & E'S Duck Dynasty & Duck Commander, N.Y. Times Bestselling Author

I.

JOURNEY 2
HEALING

CHAPTER 1

UNSPEAKABLE JOY

Rhonda Branch Ministries

Rhonda Branch Yearby, CEO LA/TX, USA

MY FAITH WAS TESTED

I was hurting because of the struggles, experiences and abuse that I have been through in my life. I continued to hurt emotionally and physically, as such, I was unable to love, to have compassion, to minister or even have a relationship with anyone and I consistently isolated myself from everyone. I needed to be Healed Badly!

They that sow in tears shall reap in Joy! Psalm 126:5

GOD REVIVED ME & REVEALED MY FAITH

As I grew and became confident in knowing God. I begin to seek out counseling and to heal from the traumas of my life! But God had a plan through all of this. God showed me how to become a conqueror. I learned how to forgive and move on, this has resulted in such **joy**. They say that the **joy** of the Lord is your strength. I know that this is true because God has placed such a **joy** in my life that I am no longer seeking to please others but rather to learn how to be all that God has called ME to be. This **joy** is unbelievable.

After many attempts to become healthy, I realized that I was destined to succeed if I was breathing. **Life is that way, sometimes you must tell your story to finish your story** I would overcome great test, and trials in my life. I overcame and continue to overcome by the blood of Jesus Christ. My faith walk is now filled with **joy** and love. I have come to know the Love of Jesus Christ. God has begun a healing process in me and continues to work through me and in me for his glory. I begin to take the word of God and build myself up, with the help of friends, family and counselors I became a healthy individual that could say "no" to abuse and "yes" to me! I realized that my life was hidden in Christ and that everything I had been through was buried with Christ and that I was raised by him to walk and live in the newness of life. God is my rock and my foundation to overcoming many obstacles and he continues to teach, lead, and guide me into all truth concerning my life. He has brought me and delivered me from the darkest places and brought me into his marvelous light. I am forever grateful to him for his faithfulness and for giving me **UNSPEAKABLE JOY!**

WORDS OF ENCOURAGEMENT

Be true to God, your faith, family & yourself! Be unique! You deserve the best and never settle for less as, you are worth so much more! Only accept **UNSPEAKABLE JOY!**

ABOUT THE AUTHOR

Rhonda Branch Yearby is a #1 International bestselling author, A successful grant writer, fundraiser, corporate/ religious event planner, songstress, & backup singer, President & CEO of Rhonda Branch Ministries. And founder of Women of Faith, Grant Seekers and BY Publishing projects of Rhonda Branch Ministries, talk show host of Keeping It REAL with Rev. Rhonda, ordained minister of the gospel, mother of 3 adult children, grandmother, great grandmother and happily married to her best friend Monroe M. Yearby, Jr.

BY Publishing's mission is to give author's a strong Christian voice and platform to teach, speak and preach to the world. **We sincerely believe that you do not have to break the piggy bank to share your story with the world and become a bestselling author!**

We provide a five-star signature, very inexpensive publishing, marketing, public relations and promotion service, we effectively assist authors to successfully publish and promote their life's works and truly connect to their friends, family and fans! We have a streamline system to launch you to a bestselling author.

BY Publishing

II.

FAITH, FAMILY, & DUCKS

CHAPTER 2

UNSHAKABLE FAITH

Miss Kay Robertson, LA, USA

Matriarch of A & E'S Duck Dynasty

MY FAITH WAS TESTED

I thought my happily-ever-after was secured the day that I married my husband. I believed marriage was beautiful and that because I was married, things would automatically be perfect! However, the marriage that I dreamed about would take a turn for the worse, and I would have to fight for what I desired in a husband and a family. My goal in life was to be the wife and the mother that God wanted me to be to my husband and children. My ultimate satisfaction could not be found in a career or success outside of my family and Jesus Christ. I would endure many trials to receive what God promised me in his word concerning my marriage and family.

My marriage was a war zone! I was in a fight for my husband and my family. This was work and there were times where I became so discouraged that I did not go to church or bible study. Even through the testing of my faith, God would remain faithful to my family. I recall an old couple taking my son to church for a period of years when I did not have the faith to continue going because I was dealing with so many other issues in my family. They would speak life into my son by telling him that he can be all that God has called him to be and saying he would preach the gospel, which he did! Even though I was struggling, I remember my boys praying for their daddy on many occasions. And they even helped me to continue to pray for my husband, even though I was separated from him for a while.

I endured many years of marital issues including addiction, drinking and infidelity. Other women would say, "he is treating you terrible, you should give up!" But I knew that I had to remain faithful to my marriage and family. I made a vow to God that I could not forsake!

GOD REVIVED ME & REVEALED MY FAITH

I took the words of my grandmother to heart. Her words were simple yet powerful! She told me to fight for my marriage and that I would have to stand and believe God. She knew that Satan would try and destroy my marriage if I allowed him because in God's word it says that Satan has come to kill, steal, and destroy. Through my grandmother's words, I developed the patience to stay with him. I knew that I had to fight the enemy no matter the circumstance! With her direction, I headed in that direction and discovered my own faith. Unshakable Faith! I began to seek the Lord wholeheartedly and to learn to trust him completely. While seeking the Lord, I developed an intimate relationship with the Lord that has remained since my faith first begin to be tested. I realized that I could not make it without the Lord and that if I trusted God to change Phil, he would do it because he is a good God that is faithful!

In life if we want to see God's hand, we must learn to trust his timing and to humble ourselves by submitting to his way and his plans. Isaiah 55:8 states, "for my thoughts *are* not your thoughts, neither *are* your ways my ways, saith the Lord." God knows exactly what each one of us are going through and he does not leave us in our mess. He specializes in fixing the things that we cannot fix on our own. He has a plan greater than anything we can think of or imagine.

As a person of faith, you cannot have your way all the time, God does not move by our demands, God moves by prayers of faith and humility. Meaning that when our faith is tried, we must be patient enough to believe God will do exactly what he promises in his word but in his timing. You can't force God's hand but you can love him enough to trust that he will never leave nor forsake you and that he will make all things work out for your good per Romans 8:28. God revealed love and faith to me through his word and continued to show forth his faithfulness to me in my marriage when I decided to freely trust him.

MY FAITH WALK TODAY

Today I can boldly declare that Jesus is the center of Phil and I's relationship. We are on the side of each other working together but God is the head of our marriage! Through many trials, we endured heartache and pain but God delivered my husband and set him free by the power of his Holy Spirit. We later renewed our "forever vows"!

We were committed to Christ and to our marriage. God honored his word by making everything work out for our good. What a blessing it was to have our son Alan marry us in front of 11 million people worldwide! God is so good!! For over 40 years Phil and I have faithfully been serving in ministry together. We have held small group bible studies in our home for over 20 years. We have assisted in helping others start their home-based bible studies and other forms of ministries. We once took a group of people to help one man to start a bible study and he is still working for the Lord faithfully today. Even when we did not have much, we remained faithful to the Lord's work by opening our small home to those that needed to hear the message of the gospel, an encouraging word and a nice hot meal!

God tells us not to despise the days of small beginnings and we surely did not! God has continuously added so much unto us! God called my husband to preach the gospel and together we have been faithful to God's calling on our life's! We have experienced many years of witnessing people give their lives to Jesus and experiencing the transformation of the gospel by becoming disciples. We learned to build disciples and to love on the broken by going to the streets and ministering to those addicted to drugs and suffering in relationships. I can recall one guy that my husband invited over for hamburgers that was a commercial fisherman. He smelled terrible!

I was somewhat annoyed by his smell until my husband reminded me that he was just a lost soul looking for acceptance. These words pierced my soul because they were true! He was just a soul that was searching for something greater than himself. You see, God doesn't require that we come to him clean or fresh., he just wants us to come! Just like that man was a fisherman, Jesus chose to use those that were dirty and stinking like fisherman. He told them to follow him and then he cleaned them up and ministered God's word to them! This was my marriage, this was my husband, this was me, and this is everyone! We all have been in a stinking mess but God chooses to use us despite us! He has used us in ministry to be a light to those that are hurting from addictions, family relationships, marriages and a host of other issues that people suffer with. Those that come are delivered from an array of issues and are healed. They learn how to be great husbands, wives, fathers, and mothers by learning from God's word. We share our own experiences with them and we help them to see that Jesus can set them free from anything! They get hope and know that things may happen but Jesus will never leave us, and Jesus will always love us!

WORDS OF ENCOURAGEMENT

Today we have a great marriage and a great family! We both have a sense of humor! We laugh about things that people normally fuss about. We put aside our pride! We apply God's word, we don't go to bed angry, we use kind words daily, and we don't look back. We have learned to enjoy life, friends, family, children and grandchildren! We have learned to live with unshakable faith that Jesus is Lord, he is powerful, and he will do all that he has promised to you!

Remember that the same power that God has in him to raise the dead, we have that same power in us! You are an overcomer!

"I can do all things through Christ which strengthens me."

– Philippians 4:13

ABOUT MISS KAY

Miss Kay Robertson is the revered matriarch of the Robertson family and star of A&E®'s *Duck Dynasty*®. She is a New York Times Best Selling Author. Kay is known for her home cooked meals and big heart! Kay loves serving her church and leader of the bible study group Muffins. She is Married to Entrepreneur Phil Robertson and the mother of 4 adult sons and daughter in laws, the grandmother of 16, and the great grandmother of 5!

III.

FAITH IN POETRY

CHAPTER 3

THE TESTING OF
FAITH POEM

Elizabeth Blade, Adelaide, Australia

We have all come to the crossroads where faith is tested. Trying times, the hard times. We somehow find our way through and in walks a different you.

The testing of time and the testing of faith. We stand the tests of time. Where everything with you gets brought out and into light. A feeling you cannot fight. From light to dark we find that inner spark.

We roam under these stars and things happen to us every single day. We bow our heads and we pray the bad times away.

We find that day; we find our faith in the in depths of our souls.

We look to the shores and we want more. The world of faith we are bound to explore.

The test that has forever being timed against us, to travel with us wherever we go. The feelings of within I know. I know that faith has tested me, I know it has tested you too.

We are bruised, used and our backs against the wall. We give ourselves away day by day for someone to hear us. The God almighty above us. The skies that run blue. The feelings of wanting and needing.

Oh, how I want you, How I want the answers to so many questions I have about me and my life. My faith has been tested, but whose hasn't? I come running back to you. The feeling of your warm and loving embrace. The feelings within in are all in place. I now know what is meant to be in this world. I know that I am meant to be, that everything in life can be a test to us. But we come running back to what we know. You shelter us from the winters rain. Wash away the agony and pain. We will meet this path again and again, but we know what is true. We will come running back to you.

REVIVE, REVEAL SO WE CAN HEAL POEM

We often search for answers in every corner of our minds, to search and want clarity in our very lives, sometimes parts within our hearts and souls dies, we must look to the ever-blue skies, call out the name to the clouds and ask to revive, heal and reveal what's inside so we can heal.

We search everything from pride to doubt we are down but not out in this world.

Parts of us close. We hold up invisible shields so no one can touch us, or find the sadden place we keep beneath us, underneath this skin and bone we can feel so alone, we walk and we roam we find what we need, we find what we desire. The never-ending search of the pits of fire.

An eternal flame, that no one is to blame, the world and life is not a game, we must look on, walk on and be strong. We must ask for guidance, we must look to you, we look to you and all that you do for answers. Life can move in mysterious ways.

Each day is different to the next, each second that passes we find ourselves wanting more, wanting and waiting for the world to explore our own inner souls and the great depths of our minds. The twisting of time and all that our life has held. We have seen miracles, we have seen the sands of the hourglass slipping through our hands, we have seen the anger and demands, but we have seen such greatness and splendor too. You have shown that to us, you have shown us the pain and the gloriousness of the beauty this world holds.

We spin forever in the world on a planet that is earth. You give birth and created anew. We are the children of you.

THE WALK OF FAITH POEM

We live, we die and we have everything in between. We have the life we lead on this earth. I am here on this walk of faith, to take the place of what I was brought here for, to make a difference with words, to send a message to you.

To hold the unglued together.

Life can be an endeavor, moments pass us by and it's the moments we forever treasure. Life goes by so quickly, the winter rain is here and gone, we hear our favorite and cherished songs. We have our first kiss, our last goodbyes.

Friendships that dwindle and divide, the thorns on our side get taken away. We bow our heads and pray. We love, we cry, we shake with madness. We feel the emptiness and sadness but we overcome it all.

Feelings that people tell you, that you're not good enough, or that you'll never make it. Feelings we try and shake it. We hear 'Fake it to you make it" but we should fake nothing, we walk on with the intent of building a vision of dreams. God has built us a kingdom and within that kingdom we stay. We show our gratitude by spreading the message of his voice. We shout it loud and proud. Feelings are shown every day and devoured. The earth and ground beneath us are soured.

But like Eagles we reel the skies, we fly above the clouds. We show ourselves on the worlds stage every single day. Bow our heads and pray that we make a breath every single day.

To the ones that has gone before us, we will remember them dearly. You have shown me the light and now I see it all clearly. The love, the trust, the bond that we have is unbreakable.

When my time is done and I climb that ladder up to the heavenly skies, I will see you Lord. I will be greeted by those that I have loved and lost, they will show me the way. I feel there love even today. They have since passed years before. Decades have passed but love gets stronger. They're my angels that watch over me now.

We can get through tough times in life, we can walk that mile and climb the highest mountain peak. If you look you shall seek, everything that you want to find in life. Set the example of those around you. Be all that you can be. Love should come to us so easily; a friendly nature should surround us wherever we go. The Lord I know will guide us through the harder times.

The heavenly light from the sun shines down on us, although the rain comes through to us, and pours on into our lives we will find our setting sun. We will run and in the fields and like a child we will run and have fun. To play for a day in the sun thanking the ultimate one.

The gift of life is what we have been given, no sense of grudges we should set forgiveness into our hearts and souls. Reach the goals and destinies of life that you have set out for yourself.

We can feel down in life, but we shall rise. The hidden surprise is in our life if we search for it. But we must want it. We must strive for it.

We must look in every part of our life. Live the life you lead, heaven wants and heaven needs. We will rejoice this is our life and our choice with choices we make. A bond with the Lord we will never break.

A love like ours is hard to find. Our bell will chime; we will face our final hour.

Every second, every day, every moment take it all in, confess to sins and know right from wrong, we all belong.

Listen to your favorite song, play the songs you play and thank the lord for today, thank your lucky stars that we get to start anew day.

So much devastation that is happening in this world, we need to find the peace as well as the peace of mind. Peace with each other and peace with ourselves.

Let your feelings glide, let them glide into the night sky, fly across the silvery moon. The glow that beams on down us at night. Say your prayers and say goodnight.

Say to yourself that everything will alright, It will. You must have faith that everything will be alright. Do what you do each day and show love and encouragement to people every day.

Show inspiration and undying love, thank the heavens above. Give a little or give a lot. You have the world in your hands.

The world is yours, do with it what you will. But never forget that you are loved and that you make a difference in this world. That is why we are here. To make a difference in someone's life and I truly believe that.

So, fly above the mountain tops and the over the oceans so blue, I am me and you are you.

ABOUT THE AUTHOR

Elizabeth Blade is from Adelaide, Australia. A writer and poet, she has co-authored several pieces two of which became international best sellers.

She has branched herself into freelance writing and has a branded name especially for her writing called Moon dance Word Artistry. She writes poems, lyrics, articles, blog pieces. Her writing is inspirational and uplifting.

She writes for needs of what people are looking for. She writes with her soul and puts her heart into everything.

Her following although small in numbers is growing larger by the day. Expanding her horizons and making connections with people all over the word.

Elizabeth is available for magazines, publications, events, special occasions, artists, musicians, individuals creating memories for loved ones and much more!

Website http://elizabethblade.com

Facebook Page: https://www.facebook.com/ElizabethBladeWriter

Twitter: https://twitter.com/Moondance_81   (@Moondance_81)

Email: moondance_81@me.com

IV.

MOTHERS &
DAUGHTERS

CHAPTER 4

A COURAGEOUS AND FAITHFUL MOTHER

Lannessa Moshay, Texas, USA

MY FAITH WAS TESTED!

My story takes place while sitting at a kitchen table. To be exact, it takes place over many kitchen tables. These kitchen tables have changed locations and styles throughout the years. Many of times, my mother was cooking and I was sitting at the table waiting to eat. There would be the rare occasion where my mother would share a little secret information into her life.

I remember sitting at the kitchen table and listening, with such great interest, to my mother talk about her experiences as a young teen mother. She surprised me with the facts of how she tried to raise both my brother, who is my senior of 1 year 9 months, and me. She had him at the young age of 15. She talked about how it was to raise him, but I do not remember much about his story as much as I remember when she introduced me into this story.

My brother was not yet 2 years of age and my mother was now a young expecting mother. She told of how she was scared and alone. At the age of 17, my mother is now a mother of two little children under the age of 2.

Sitting at the table watching Mom stay busy as she talks helps to keep me engaged. She is doing her favorite past time, cooking. Fried chicken I believe was the dish. As she imparted this new-found information, she cleaned the chicken. She would drop a new twist-and-turn of her young, not yet adult life. She moved to the counter where she had prepared her seasoning and batter. I quickly thought, oooh I cannot wait to get my piece, yet, I did not want to interrupt her train of thought. This was a rare moment of sharing between my mother and me.

As I listen, in awe, to my mom tell her story I think about how challenging it must have been to be a teen because let's face it adolescent years are awkward times alone. To make growing up more challenging, add pregnancy to the equation. As Mom talked, my mind raced at the speed of light at these numerous thoughts: how come she did not have any help? Where were her parents? Wait her parents were and are my grandparents. She was not the only child. Where were her brothers, my uncles? There had to have been a daddy... The big thought that captured my heart (and I am so grateful for the outcome, yet still) is that she could have aborted me. Both of us could have suffered this ill fate. We were not making her life easier. She was still a teenager trying to figure out life alone, but with two little babies.

When I snapped out of my thoughts, it was like I never missed a word because; I remember hearing Mom tell about the next sequential thing that happened. As I ate my hot fried chicken I listened intently to her talk about how she raised two little babies alone. She talked about having to make hard decisions that made her cry on a nightly basis. She talked about the hard questions she had to answer with her actions, actions that would be courageous, yet scary.

Do you leave your children home to pursue your high school diploma? Who are we to say, "I would not do that? That sounds like a horrible thing to do." Nevertheless, the alternative was worse by not creating a better life for the babies. Hearing this is shocking, but inspiring at the same time. My mother told that her heart broke every night. She had to leave us asleep in the crib with a bottle.

She would pray over us and ask God to please keep us safe. She would close the door and walk at night to the Catholic Church across the street to attend class. She worked hard to get her General Education Diploma. Now, I heard this I felt proud of my mommy. She pushed through a large obstacle many times and did it although it was hard and she was seemingly unsupported. Not only did she press to get her GED, she persevered to earn and receive her Massey Business School certificate. Just imagine her pride in telling me about how she received her certificate.

Let's advance some years from my infancy to childhood.

One story I remember, I was sitting at the kitchen table during a big storm. It was one of the storms that made a mark in the 1980's. I remember the scene as if I were sitting at the kitchen table right at this moment. My older brother and I were sitting out of order. Meaning, we were not in our regular chairs. Well, at least he was not. This night I sat to his right. Our mom was standing closest to him. She was trying to figure what to feed us. The lights blew out. Although the stove was gas, Mom would not turn on the stove. "To make things fun, we will light these candles", I remembered she would say this many of times when the lights were out (not always due to the storm). That is another faith story and book. Mom pulled out cans of Vienna sausages and Spam.

I did not appreciate either however; I did not appreciate hunger pains more. She asked which did we prefer and opened our cans. I was excited because we had the white square crackers and eating by candlelight was a big treat. Although the storm was loud, the trees swayed real hard, the shutters made lots of noise and the lights were out - it became okay.

In these moments, the storm became silent for me because my mom was right there. She told us we would be okay because God will take care of us. I didn't have a full grasp of Who God was but He must be good because Mom always said so. She was not showing any fear; therefore, we took on her energy. I can say, as I look back now, that those times are seeds of faith God was using to plant into me. They were seeds to trust in Him, His abilities and Who He is.

Time passed and I recall sitting next to another type of table during this new faith seed implantation. I am now at least the age of 8 or 9 years. I am the new big sister to a little cute baby brother. He was in the toddling stage. He just started pulling himself up to a standing position. He toddled and bobbed about a lot. The three of us were out with our mom. She was visiting a friend. I honestly do not remember the lady, but I do remember her brown wooden coffee table. It was shaped like a hexagon with a glass center. I also remember two significant things that happened around that table.

The first recollection was hearing God speak to me telling me I would remember this day. My immediate thought was, "what's so significant about *this* day". Now, here I am, thirty-plus years later, and typing this memory. The second memory could have changed our lives forever. We are sitting on the floor playing quietly, ever so often looking at the baby to make sure he was playing happily. I saw an ashtray that I wanted to remove because it had cigarette butts in it. I knew not to touch it because Momma did not play that. We were trained to not touch other people's things. At the time, I did not know how significant that desire to move that ashtray would be.

Momma was sitting nearby talking to her friend, when God clearly spoke to me to look at my baby brother. I didn't think anything of it as it sounded to me like a regular thought to just check on the baby. I looked over at him and he was eating the cigarette butts. I gasped loud enough to get my mom's attention. She looked in our direction but her friend looked and dismissed the situation. I told my mom in a loud demanding voice to see the baby. He needed her.

She immediately saw he was gasping for air. His mouth was full of the cigarette butts. It was horrible to see. I could tell my mom was scared as she was fishing all the butts out of his mouth while telling him to breathe. I immediately started to pray and ask, "Dear God please breathe through the baby." I prayed that He would please let the baby breathe again. I did honestly believe that God would do it. I did not know the word "faith" yet, but I did believe the same God who calmed the storm we experienced earlier could breathe air back into my little brother. I am glad to tell you my brother lived. His breath came back to him and he cried a little but he was just fine. Another seed planted inside me that God would use at another date. God is the breath of life. Genesis 2:7 and Job 33:4 both reference God as the Almighty One, who breathes life into man's nostrils and gives life. Thank you, God, for Jesus!

Not sure why God wants to share this tad bit of information but in hopes that it would encourage parents to listen to and protect their children's moral excellence and innocence. This is another table I found myself sitting. This one was out of sheer discomfort. I sat as a preteen at my mom's friend house. She was nice enough but her children were "_____". My brothers and I were invited to spend the night while my mother went to work that night. As a child, this sounded like fun. We had a blast playing with them throughout the day; however, there was a different feel at their home at night. The family had possibly 8 people living in a 2-bed room apartment. The lady's children ranged from very young to 20's. Everything was well the earlier part of the evening. We all found a comfortable spot on the floor and fell asleep.

As a light sleeper, I quickly opened my eyes to someone trying to open my jean pants. Oh no! What do I do? I laid there frozen in movement, but my mind raced at a million miles a second. I just couldn't get my body to move away to safety. After what seemed like hours, but was only minutes, I finally could muster up a "God help me get out of here" prayer. "Please give me courage to run". I moved a little, and then God said, "I gave you the strength and courage; you have to move on your own." I got up and I stepped over all the bodies on the floor and walked down the hall to the living room. As I made my way in there, I saw the man's mom. The man was one of the older teen / young adult sons. He was tall especially to me; I was possibly 10 or 11. When I saw his mother, I thought, yes, I am safe. She was sitting at the kitchen table smoking a cigarette. Although I hate the smell and the smoke of a cigarette I looked past that to talk with her. I went to her believing I would find safety, the same kind, like in my mother's arms. Like when there is a storm and my mom would tell me it would be okay. Hoping she would tell me to trust in God and He will deliver me from evil. Tell me something!

However, Ms. Lady, (I don't recall her name) did not believe me or just did not want to believe me what I told her had transpired a few minutes a few feet away from her. As I talked with her I realized she didn't want the truth. She told me to "prove he tried to touch me". I looked at her bewildered, like how do you "prove it". My mind raced through the whole encounter in the room and *how* she was talking to me then I let her have it. The flood gates opened and I cried and cried and cried. My tears had no end. I just kept calling for my mother to be placed on the phone. I wanted my mommy. I didn't want anything she had to offer anymore. She reluctantly dialed the number then handed me the phone. She did not want to talk to my mom, her "friend". It was so hard to muster up the strength to form words that expressed - "come get me now, Mom."

My mom could have had a super cape when she arrived because she came. I mean SHE CAME! It took a lot for my mom to get to me. First, she did not have a car - the one reason she could not get to me at the hour I called. She had to wait until the city bus began to run again.

Although Ms. Lady lived in an apartment on the second floor, I could vividly see my mom walk through the court yard downstairs. My insides became happy because as she had arrived and the sun was literally coming over the horizon.

Once my mommy came, the atmosphere and attitudes changed. Ms. Lady changed her tune to a helpful nice tune toward me. She was no longer rude, cold, or calculating toward me, but soft spoken and kind. She was sympathetic and eager to share my details with my mother. The same details she told me I was lying about. The same details for which she frowned at me.

I look back now and think that is one table I never want to see or sit at again. That table had bad memories and bad people.

Please allow me to encourage you to walk faithfully with God with this last input. I have been tested many times in my faith, from the age of a youth and beyond my young adult years. As a child, I have seen God provide manna for our family. My young mother, older brother and I were homeless (although, I did not know it). We were privileged to stay inside a Salvation Army, a hotel or a safe place. I just remember my Mom telling us that God would take care of us - so I believed her. Although we shared a dinner table with seemed to be a hundred other mothers with children, it was good for my heart to do it with my mommy.

As a young adult, I prayed to the same God to provide for me once again as He provided places for me to live as a child. After a not-so-good relationship went bad I needed a place to stay immediately. I had no job, no savings and to make it more challenging, I was a first-generation college student fighting to complete my senior year. God not only provided a place for me to stay, but He did it without me having to make compromises. (You know the kind that makes you feel like you have sold yourself to the devil.) I was truthful with the apartment managers and God moved through them to open their doors to me. I am a believer that God provides for those who trust and believe in His Word. He has promised to take care of His children and I am proof that He continues to do so.

When I think about all the things God has delivered me from and brought me to, I know that I can have faith in Him and His Word. He is not a mere man. He will never tell a lie. He will not make any mistakes. If I place my trust in His abilities and not my own, I will not be put to shame.

I sit here today, a wife of a righteous man and a mother of three little gentlemen. Now it is my turn to provide protection, to instill Godly wisdom and to teach about having faith in God. At my table, I am intentional. I teach our sons school lessons, Bible Scriptures, etiquette and how to become Godly men and husbands who can cook. Good food always makes my soul happy.

At this same table, God uses me to encourage younger ladies looking for marriage and parenting advice. As I serve my family and get our home in order, God has allowed doors to be opened for both my husband and I to minister to couples and me to mothers and wives. This just shows me how His Word has come alive in my life. Proverbs 18:6 NASB states, "A man's gift makes room for him…" or as the Message Bible states it, "A gift gets attention." 1

As a woman of faith, my encouragement to you is to expect God to do what He says. He expects us to do our part. He knows life will happen, the course will get bumpy, and you will become discouraged. Nevertheless, as God wipes away your tears, He expects you to get back on course. He expects you to complete what He has begun in you.

There I was once again at a table making life alterable plans. This time, it wasn't at the kitchen table. I sat at a very small table in front of my plane seat. In my new level of faith, today, I stand believing God will use our family to create a conference to make and train children disciples. God spoke to me through my experiences in South Africa which was enough to trust Him and move forward. As we stand in faith waiting on Him to move on the conference's behalf, we continue to pray. This has never been done before. (Like Noah's Ark – it had never rained before). The vision is BIG. It is real BIG. God left no blueprints to follow just some ideas downloaded into my heart as I crossed the Atlantic Ocean. Knowing God is the true provider, I will have what He has given me the vision to pursue.

I will have victory in all situations. This is the totality of my faith in our great BIG God.

Lannessa Moshay, her husband and three sons have co-founded The BIG 5 Ministries. www.TheBIG5Conference.com the premier children conference, a non-profit, commissioned to make and train children disciples. Children and women focused, Lannessa is glocal (global and local) minded and have shared the Gospel in 4 countries, 3 Continents and multiple cities and states. As the head DiVA of Pregnant DiVAS (www.PregnantDiVAS.com) Lannessa has spoken on parenting panels and privately empowers mothers to nurture their young. While home schooling, she spends quality hours teaching her sons Bible doctrine and to become Godly husbands.

For engagements, Lannessa may be reached at DiVAS@PregnantDiVAS.com.

CHAPTER 5

TRUST IN THE LORD

Kay Mitchum, West Monroe, La, USA

MY FAITH WAS TESTED

Between 10 to 12 years ago, I knew that the mother that I had was not the mother that I grew up knowing. I was struggling to accept that my mother was struggling with her health. This was very difficult for me as a woman that grew up with such a loving and tender mother. She was sick to the point that her personality was changing. Mom had Alzheimer's disease and was in the early stages of dementia. This would ultimately change my life. As a daughter, I knew that I had to care for my mother. So, I made the necessary adjustments to help her overcome her health condition.

After I found my mother was sick, I made the preparations to see that she had care 24/7. God made a way for me to take care of her while I was at work as a nurse. My administrator allowed me to take my mother to work with me on the weekends and days that I did not anyone to look after her. Although this was a great emotional strain for me, I knew that it was my duty to care for my mother. As my mom grew ill, I knew that I would not be able to keep up the trend of caring for her while I worked. The Lord started to deal with me about leaving my job. This was difficult for me because this would mean that I would no longer have a 6-figure salary and would have to sacrifice the luxurious things in life that I had become accustomed to as a career woman. I even loved my job as a nurse administrator but I had to learn to trust in the Lord, this was difficult for someone like me that was always used to working. This was the point in my life where I had to realize that my plans were not the Lord's plans. Isaiah 55:8 states, "For my thoughts *are* not your thoughts, neither *are* your ways my ways, saith the LORD." This is what the Lord wanted me to do, I knew that if I followed his plans, I would be alright.

With much prayer and after finding out that I needed a knee replacement, I decided to leave my job. After a knee replacement, I was worried about who would care for my mother because I had to go through physical therapy. This was a step of faith for me as a woman that was always used to working and I would have to depend solely on the Lord in all areas of my life. I knew that this was the will of God and the plan of God for me to take care of my mother and from that moment forward I trusted God enough to care for her. With little finances, a handicapped leg, and a heart to do what was right, I took care of her from that point on.

GOD REVIVED ME AND REVEALED MY FAITH

After the Lord revealed faith to me, I could completely depend on him. I never knew just how much God would provide all my needs until I was not able to do it all on my own. He has been my source of strength and God has been providing for me from the very start. I learned to cut back on the things that I did not need. If I went to the movies last week, I did not need to go this week, and if I got my hair done every two weeks, I did not need to get it done this week. The strength of my life was in my power to say no to the things that I did not need. I started to deny myself of things that I wanted to do the things that I needed to do for my mother. I knew that God would always provide for me. I learned to rely on him 24/7. The Lord revealed to me that I was his daughter and that he would ALWAYS take care of me. If God would provide with a job, then God would take care of me without a job. God knew that I had to care for my mom, therefore, he would not let us go without!

MY FAITH WALK TODAY

My faith walk today is strong. I have learned to trust the Lord. Trusting the Lord is needed in faith. I have learned that no matter what, God will be God and that he has a plan for all that he allows. My prayer is that I would be prepared to let go of my mom when she passes away. I also have been praying that I would not have to take my mom go to a nursing home and that she will not remember us as she continues to age. Allow her to have a peaceful death without suffering. That I would have the faith to understand that God will be God and that he will always cause things to work out for my good.

WORDS OF ENCOURAGEMENT

My encouragement for anyone that is dealing with an illness is to accept it in old age. God knows best and that God will always bring you through. If it got you from A to B, he will get you from B to C. Trust in the Lord with all thine heart and lean not unto your own understanding, in all your ways acknowledge him and he shall direct your path! Believe him and watch what he can do.

ABOUT THE AUTHOR

Kay Mitchum was born November 8, 1951. She came from a family of educators; her mother and father were among the first in the state of Texas to work in integrated schools. She received her BS in nursing from Baylor University. She has been a nurse since 1975 and is the mother of a daughter and the grandmother of 1. She relocated and now lives in Louisiana. She is retired and plans to go to back to work soon to continue to pursue her passion for medicine. Her hobbies include spending time with family and friends, going to the mall and pool exercising. She is known for her love for people and does what she can for anybody that needs encouragement or help. Scripture to stand on by Faith I can do all things through Christ that strengthens me. Philippians 3:14

Contact Ms. Kay Mitchum @ kayfmicthum@icloud.com

CHAPTER 6

DANCING IN THE DARK

Deborah Hegre, Connecticut, USA

MY FAITH WAS TESTED

For years, I searched for GOD. I was raised a Catholic and received every Sacrament. My Mother made sure that I stay close to the nun and church. At sixteen my Mother wanted me to go to a Convent to become a nun. She felt that if would keep me safe.

My Mother was raped by three men at the age of thirteen and when I was born she had it in her mind to always protect me. I think that is why she wanted me to be a nun. I really don't know; other than she wanted it so badly. My Mother became a widow at 24. She was left with no insurance; no money and a 12-year-old child to raise. We went to live with my Grandmother and then Mom had a nervous breakdown and I didn't see her for almost a year.

GOD REVIVED ME & REVEALED MY FAITH!

Living with my Grandmother wasn't easy. I had to help her with my Great Grandmother who was steadily complaining that she was going to die daily. I guess my GOD reveal my faith at that time was to continue to believe in him and that Mom would be home soon and we could be a family again. I didn't know much about faith or how to get it at the time. Catholics really don't focus on that. I lived with praying to statues and the lighting of candles to answer prayer. I went to Sunday school and participated in all the church events; but I felt empty. I loved Jesus and didn't approve of having to see him still being on the cross. He came to earth to free us. He allowed himself to be beaten and nailed to a cross; all for us.

I believed; that is when faith steps in. I had faith but it was so small. My Mom would tell me that even if your faith is as small as a mustard seed; God accepts that.

MY FAITH WALK TODAY

I don't know when my faith walk started. I know that I was searching for the real God the one that I could have a close relationship with.

My first marriage my husband was very abusive. He did not keep a job and it took great faith to be able to take care of my Son and my Mother. I took my Mom in so we could take care of her and she could watch my Son while I worked. I thought this was the way life should be. A man that was too lazy to care for his family; but I kept my vows and stayed. Then the physical abuse came. That was when I decided to leave with my Son and my Mother. We moved into a nice apartment but the toll that the marriage took with me I became very ill and couldn't work for a while. I always heard that still small voice in my head telling me that I could do it.

I usually sat their bible in hand and empty. Then depression started to move in on me. I had my bible but was still lost and without God. I remember waking up during the night and felt a hand on my shoulder. I saw someone in white in the corner of my room when I napped, at night that shadow was there. I attributed it to the shadows I had seen as a child.

For several years, I fell away from church. My life was increasing getting worse and my second Husband started abusing me; and shortly after about a year into the marriage he was arrested for assault. I thought to myself; where is God? Again, I had no real faith to speak of. I was broken and lost. I started to go to the clubs on the base. I didn't do anything wrong I did it to get out and feel like someone. I thought if I challenged God he would appear to me. For more than 10 years I left out reading my bible and didn't think of God at all. I went through several years of depression and

I continued to attend the church and became one of the churches favorite people. I would cook and clean and do everything that I was asked to do. I still had no faith or maybe just a little. I had faith I just didn't think that I did.

I continued to teach Sunday school but no matter what I did for the church I stayed empty and sad inside. They taught about God, Jesus and they talked about faith but it was like a light was out inside of me. That is when God started to talk to me. At night, he would wake me at 2 or 3 am and ask me to get up and pray. He sometimes would tell me who to pray for these people I didn't know but God would show me them through the Holy Spirit.

Late 2013 was the time of rejoicing and where I accepted Jesus with my whole heart and gave my life to him. I then began to read scripture and witness to people. I began to hold spiritual counseling for friends and their friends. The depression subsides and I began to sing the Lord's praises and continue to walk in faith. Over the past 4 years I have been in some bad situations because I didn't pray first. But God was always there. In one of my bad choices I went to live in Florida with family.

They told me to go and I was looking at sleeping outside the Salvation Army on a mat. I prayed to God for a miracle and within 24 hours I had money and was headed back to Connecticut. I drove for four days with no sleep and very little food. On the last day, I was out of insulin, but God got me back safe and I am sure that he was with me the entire time.

WORDS OF ENCOURAGEMENT

The only thing I can say is that when we are at our weakest he is strong. I would suggest that you never lose faith and always know that God is near. He will never leave us or forsake us; never. When we feel alone he is never far from us. Jeremiah 29:11 His promises is for the best for us because he loves us.

A few months ago, I was battling with my finances. My Aunt had given me a ring and I cherished it. But with the ring came a lot of sorrow and I grew to resent it. Some of my family believed strongly in generational curses. I then struggled for quite some time. My Aunt told me one day that she witnessed my Great Grandmother removing a growth from an Aunt's stomach. She is a born again Christian and still believes in curses. We had a conversation about it and I told her to pray to God to remove that thought from her mind. I told her that thoughts were not from God but the enemy. I prayed all that night for her release.

The day that I was to take the ring to sell I was so full of fear about it. I stopped and prayed to God. I told him that he knew how much fear that I had and I needed to get rid of this ring that brought me pain. When I went to the jeweler I had so much calm and after I sold the ring I didn't think about the ring anymore and drove home with so much peace and release. God said he will never leave us. He has proven true so many times in my life and he will do that for you too. If you have an issue you want release from. Just trust in God and have faith. Even if it is as small as a mustard see.

ABOUT THE AUTHOR

Deborah Hegre resides in Connecticut. She works as caregiver for elderly individuals. and meet people. She accepted a work assignment at 20 hours a week working with elderly individuals. Deborah is an avid reader and has just partnered with the local library on developing writing programs. Deborah is working with local colleges to hold meetings for Domestic Abuse Survivors; that is her passion. Deborah is also a Domestic Violence Survivor. She has suffered more than 40 years of Domestic Violence hegredjs@hotmail.com.

V.

FAITH IN
FASTING

CHAPTER 7

MOUNTAIN MOVING FAITH

Tameka Jordan, LA, USA

MY FAITH WAS TESTED

So many times, as a woman you can face unexpected challenges that are unbearable. Thus, you can begin to depreciate life. I'm a living witness to the many trials, tribulations, and unexpected situations that we, as women, face. In 2002, my life went from a life of stability to being shaken all in a blink of an eye. I loss a baby that I desperately wanted, my doctor found lumps in each of my breast, I was on the verge of losing my job, and my grades began to fall. My world seemed like it was falling apart and I felt like giving up! This is when I came to the realization that my faith was being tested. I prayed consistently about my situation, but I was still lacking something in those prayers.

GOD REVIVED ME & REVEALED MY FAITH

I was reminded of some advice that my former pastor always gave to the church about praying sincerely and having faith that what you pray shall come to past. His favorite scripture was "Walk by Faith, Not by Sight". After being reminded of this, I immediately dropped to my knees and begin to pray! I prayed for unshakable faith, for closure, for healing, and for strength mentally, physically, and emotionally. After weeks of praying with sincerity, God revealed to me the word, "fast." Fasting was something that I heard of growing up in the church, but it was something that I personally never experienced. Despite my inexperience with fasting, I was obedient and followed his request and I fasted.

Due to my amateurishness about fasting, I begin to seek accurate information through various resources, in which I did obtain enough information concerning the subject. In fact, I complied bible scriptures along the way in my study time. Those scriptures led me to the Word of God, where I found reliable information, and confirmation was given and received.

After many hours of reading and interpreting, I was finally awakened to the profound meaning of fasting. A week later, I begin to frequently fast and faithfully pray. I did this for weeks, but it was like I was devoting all my time to God by sincerely praying and fasting for nothing, because my pain and trials seemed like they were getting worst. But, something just wouldn't allow me to lose hope. I begin to pray even harder. I asked God for guidance. I recalled the idiom that "Prayer is the key and FAITH unlocks the door". I then realized that I was praying and fasting, but faith and patience was not present.

God worked in a higher way than I thought! The very next time I opened my bible, I was led to Thessalonians 5:17 "Pray without ceasing" and then I was led to Matthew: 21-22, "And whatever you ask in prayer, you will receive, if you have faith". Along the way, I was guided to 2 Peter 3:9 which paraphrases that "There are things in your life right now that are trying your patience." Those three scriptures gave me a better view and a clear understanding of faith. Patience was something that didn't come naturally for me, so I begin to pray for it. This time, I prayed but before I got finished, something on the inside of me said, "cast all your problems to God and leave them there." This, of course, was something different, but again I was obedient. Not even two weeks into being obedient to God's request is when I begin to feel comfortable and the pain begin to slowly cease. I was no longer thinking, wondering, or imagining things of the past.

Though I felt revived, I consistently surrendered and submitted myself to God. God spoke to me again and said, "I will give you another child, in due time. I immediately became mentally healed. When the doctors informed me that my lumps were benign. I was immediately physically healed. My job was no longer at risk, and my grades started to gradually ascend. At this point, I was not only emotionally healed, but I had a renewed mind and I regained hope for tomorrow. My worries had ceased and my tears were all cried out. My breakdown became a breakthrough and, at this point, I was finally able to say I was revived from all my existing troubles.

MY FAITH WALK TODAY

Today, I still faithfully pray, fast, and have bold faith along with endless patience. I was blessed with a son that God promised and even blessed to have a precious daughter. I'm currently healed and healthy. I'm a 4.0 student with a purpose. As a woman that's been through the storm, whenever a storm occurs in my life, I just kneel on my knees and pray. As a woman of God, I'm a firm believer that we face obstacles as a test and that our faith will be on trial. As a woman of patience, I wait on God to fix the situation. As a woman of faith, I don't give up. As a woman of faith, I praise him even during my hardest times in life. Now that I'm acquainted with God and his power, I never feel hopeless or give up because he can fix any situation in life. I've learned that patience is necessary in so many situations, but faith makes all things possible. As I conclude, women whenever you're going through the storm chose faith over doubt, faith over fear, faith over the unseen. Never think, wonder, imagine, or obsess; instead, kneel and pray. Lastly, never lose courage in considering your own imperfection. Worrying ends when faith in God begins.

WORDS OF ENCOURAGEMENT

Have faith and never give up and the Lord will see you through!

ABOUT THE AUTHOR

Tameka Jordan is a freelance writer who resides in Monroe, La. But is from Sicily Island, La, where the population is at few, but their praise for God is never overdue. She attends Grambling State University, where she's a 4.0 scholar pursuing her Master's degree in Criminal Justice. Last but certainly not least, she attends True Vine Baptist Church, where they are Learning, Loving, and Learning God. Furthermore, she's a Woman of God with bold faith and unspeakable joy.

VI.

FAITH IN SUCCESS & YOURSELF

CHAPTER 8

WE CAN DO ALL THINGS THROUGH CHRIST

Katrina M. Walker Texas, USA

MY FAITH WAS TESTED

My mother was a woman that loved the Lord and taught me a lot of things. Shortly after she had me, she married a military man. We would live all over the country and over the world. This built in me an appreciation for culture and the arts. I had the opportunity to be in a break dancing competition in California and, won The Ford Motor Company Award. I became a cheerleader in Germany that lead to many competitions and a boot camp experience with the Dallas Cowboy Cheerleaders. However, not everything was perfect! Our blended family had conflict and trouble. Many things transpired because of my step- father's actions. The things that took place in our household during his tenure were devastating to my mother and I for years to come.

After he and my mom were separated, we moved back to the states after being stationed in a foreign country for a while. It was in between these times where I would grow a deeper love for dance. I had been dancing since I was around 2 years old but in high school I developed my craft in dance. It just so happened that I was blessed to audition for a major rap group from Dallas. That's how I started dancing and touring.

However, I was still living at home and had a part time job while I was still in high school. I was helping at home, but things changed at home and me being a teenager and not wanting to follow my mother's rules I left home. This is how my faith was tested and my journey into adulthood begin. I moved with nothing when I left. I moved in with a guy friend that I was in love with, but in a short amount of time that ended. I knew I had to stand on my own two feet, so I got a stable job and a car. I perfected my art as a dancer and eventually became a professional dancer.

This was always a dream of mine many of my friends and family always told me how talented I was at the art of dance. I would dance for big name stars in the 90s like Vanilla Ice. These were some of the people that I toured with and that wanted me to travel with them. 90s Rapper like Apache Clan etc. Wanted me to be a part of their dance crew as well. In the mist of all the excitement and traveling and, meeting famous people, while I was dancing I was dating.

I fell in love with a rapper who I danced with for a long duration of time. During the tenure of that relationship I became pregnant with his child. This would seem like a mistake to many but the Lord opened my eyes to see that no matter the circumstances he always works things out for our good. Once again, my faith in the Lord was tested After I found out that I was pregnant, I heavily debated the choice between going on tour with R Kelly and Salt and Pepper 1993 tour or keeping my baby. Right before I found out that I was pregnant, I was offered to go on tour with a major artist as an official dancer for their dance team. This was a difficult thing for me because I had worked so hard to get to that level that I wanted to be at, I wanted to dance so much that I dropped out of high school to pursue dancing full time.

After contemplating everything that was going on in my life, I decided to keep the baby. It was not hard for me to make that decision after I had an image of my child growing older, it is amazing how God can show you the image of something and it can change the destination of your life and journey with God and how the holy spirit will reveal once you prayed and he directs your footsteps. I chose to have my baby and gave birth to a beautiful baby girl. My daughter's father and I were both young and not prepared for parenthood.

He and I lived together for much of our relationship 10 years. My faith begins in my journey with womanhood and motherhood. God has a funny way of showing us in your darkest days and in the happiest moments he is there all the time. 365 days, He is there when we call his name. My family helped and I worked and so did her father but I had worked until the day that I had her. I was employed at the warehouse that her dad worked at as well. we had a one bedroom apartment but when she came he was not ready to give up his lifestyle for his child.

He was not ready to be a parent or father so this left me with the sole responsibility of having to care for the family and finding better employment. Since I did not finish high school it was difficult for me to make ends meet with several dead-end jobs. I was a very ambitious person that was met with some unexpected roadblocks, however, I did not let the troubles I was facing stop me. I worked and I studied for my GED and I took the test once and passed the test with flying colors! After that I went to college for Information Technology and received several certifications and worked as IT Tech. My faith was tested daily in my motherhood and parenting because I would have to believe God for the essential needs for my daughter and myself. I would have to hustle to make sure that she had clothes and all her necessary items.

Although it seemed as if I had given up much of my life to raise my daughter, God would begin to slowly restore me through the process of growing with her. I lost faith in my dreams and aspirations but I gained much more through motherhood.

GOD REVIVED ME & REVEALED MY FAITH!

God answers every call in his time and he always answers in the right timing as well. It seems like you may struggle to get to a place for a while but in that struggling you learn so much that it almost seems necessary to stay prayed up and keep an open amour of God, faith, and hope. The trials and tribulations will pass and after it is over you overcome, the lesson. I thought my boyfriend was ready to settle down but we both were very immature.

After getting a home and him asking me to marry him it just didn't work out as planned and I ended up working two jobs and trying take care of my daughter and the household which eventually I ended up leaving. I stepped out on faith and left the relationship to raise her on my own. I stayed close so they could have a relationship. I raised her with God's help and assistance from both sides of the families. His family had also always been supportive of me.

However, my daughter changed me the day she came into my life. I become a mother and that was the most humbling experience of my life. It was as if God used her as a tool to make me grow up. I instantly knew that I needed better for myself and that I wanted better the day that she was born. God began to show me that I had to do better in choosing people in my life and in my circle, that I needed to show her what it meant to be a true woman of faith and what it means to serve the Lord. I did not become perfect the day that she came into my life but I did learn to love unconditionally and sacrificially. God revealed faith to me through my daughter. Having a baby changes your perspective on life and my daughter certainly changed mine.

So, after staying with my baby's father for a long time, I decided to leave him and continue living my life. I wanted to give her the opportunities to became the best person she could be and instill her with the faith I had learned and to keep God first. I wanted to ensure that my daughter understood how important an education was and that she had great friends that could help to keep her grounded in the right direction. This was not easy but God began to reveal to me how to be a good parent and how to love her unconditionally without spoiling her. My faith increased more.

My daughter helped me to see that I deserved better as a woman and to set that example for her as a mother. God revealed that I did not need a man to be happy but that my happiness was connected to him! I showered her with unconditional love. I focused on her and building her up to be all that God called her to be. This was a faith walk daily to me. My own mother even helped me to see my worth as a woman and to understand that I was becoming a new person on the inside. My mother and grandmother and the women of my family were leaders and I desired to walk their footsteps and take their advice and prayers and along with that they financially helped me with daughter I never asked for assistance they just did it because I was a hard-working single mother and that is what family does to support you in your faith walk. God showed me how to overcome the worries of this life and to focus on him as my sole provider concerning my daughter and me.

MY FAITH WALK TODAY

The Lord did see us through it all. He took us from victory to victory and God has been the sole person that taught me how to raise my daughter. Today I have a job that pays well working in IT. I also went back to school to obtain further education to be successful in life. I have successful relationships with my friends and I have healthy relationships with much of my intermediate family. I also have developed in my faith walk by attending church regularly, praying and reading my bible. As, I was taught growing up.

I learned how to pray for all that I need and how to wait on God for the manifestation of what I need from his word. The Lord has loved me when no one else would and he has kept me from many dangers on the course of my journey. However, the biggest accomplishment that I can say I have had in my life, is by raising a beautiful daughter that has grown up to be an inspiration to many. My daughter is not only a high school graduate, but she holds a degree in Architecture from Prairie View A&M University. She does not have any children and recently took an internship to Australia for architecture.

The Lord has been faithful to my daughter and me. He provided her with scholarships and I worked hard to provide her with a car. God has done all this through his son Jesus Christ. I know that without the Lord, I would not be who I am and what I am today. I am thankful every day for all that he has done in my life. I love the Lord and I know that I have not seen the end of his goodness in my life and in the life of those around me.

WORDS OF ENCOURAGEMENT

I would like to encourage women around the world to love themselves no matter what. Do not accept anything in life and do not allow anyone abuse or misuse you because you are worth so much more. Give all your problems to God and learn to love yourself because God loves you! Trust him in the difficult times because I know that he will see you through.

ABOUT THE AUTHOR

Katrina M. Walker is an IT professional, semi-professional soccer player and the proud mother of one daughter, Kyna Boyd who is currently working on her master's degree in Architecture. Katrina is an author. She has a passion for dance and loves to spend time with her family and friends. Contact Information: https://www.katrinawalkerfrombrokentounbreakable.wordpress.com Email Katrina @ kwalker1127@gmail.com

CHAPTER 9

JOURNEY TO WHOLENESS

Ashley Kennedy – Natchitoches, LA, USA

MY FAITH WAS TESTED

I was born in a small town in Louisiana and raised in an era where it wasn't uncommon for your grandmother to be the head of the household. This was the story of my life. Both of my parents suffered from life-changing events that ultimately became the cause of their absence within my life. Many of my peers, seemed to also have absentee parents because of drug addictions, incarcerations, death, work/business, abuse, etc.

Like I said, it wasn't uncommon for your grandmother to be the head of the household. However, this was a difficult thing for me to cope with. Although I had a great upbringing, because of the love extended from my grandmothers, I often felt alone and dealt with the spirit of rejection because of the absence of my parents. I spent half of my childhood in Natchitoches, Louisiana with my maternal grandmother. It was in this small town, that she gave me the biggest gift I've ever received.......... she taught me how to PRAY! She showed me how to "Wait on the Lord", how important it is to keep forgiveness in my heart and to never be ashamed of where/ who I come from. At the age of eleven, I moved to Inkster, Michigan to live with my paternal grandmother, where the joy was beyond overwhelming.

Family functions surrounded by 4 generations of genuine love! Sounds fulfilling, right? Should have been, but even as good as family "felt", I still wasn't emotionally healed and the disconnect with my parents became more difficult for me, and it simply wasn't enough. I kept quiet most of the time, not knowing how to deal with many of my thoughts towards myself and my parents. Smiling to hide the pain. Laughing to keep from crying. It's easy to cover-up a battle when you have no physical scars.

I did not understand a lot of the reasons that I felt the way that I felt. But I knew that if I wanted to overcome it all, I had to, "PRAY, FORGIVE and give it to God." Cliché, right? As predictable as it may appear, it is truly the necessary steps to overcoming feelings of hurt, depression, abandonment and many other spiritual battles. It wasn't until I began to pray for God to give me a clean heart, and renew in me a right mind that I began to view my parents as human begins, whom is guilty of sin and falling short, just as I, that I began to flourish. Understanding the URGENCY OF FORGIVENESS saved my life. I began to LIVE after I FORGAVE.

GOD REVIVED ME & REVEALED MY FAITH

At the age of 21, I moved back to Louisiana. At the time, I was spiritually empty. Discourage from dropping out of college, I was anything but excited about the journey that was ahead of me. I had become so wrapped up in a lifestyle that was never meant for me. Dating all the wrong guys, befriended all the wrong friends, partying all the time, ABANDONING my relationship with GOD. I went from 0 to 100 quick, and I don't mean in a good way.

Those 4 years after high school had completely slipped through my fingers, BECAUSE I TOOK MY FOCUS OFF GOD AND HIS PURPOSE FOR MY LIFE. It is easy to fall victim to distractions, when your prayer life isn't consistent. The enemy has a way of tempting you into situations and circumstances that will drag you down if you are not spiritually equipped.

I then began to PRAY and ask God to give me a spirit of discernment to spot my distractions and hide me from anything that would deter me from his will. I was not at all sure what God was going to do in my life but I put my trust in Him and He began to heal my past and write my future. I enrolled in cosmetology school and found my passion for art and creativity. It was through my gift that I realized, even though I may have failed at some things in life, that did not mean that I was a failure. God broke my chains of rejection and he helped me to overcome discouragement in the areas of my life that I felt were broken.

After graduation, I happened to get a job at the first salon I entered! (When God is involved, He'll make your steps plain) I only worked at the nail salon for a year and eleven months. Not even two years into my new career and I was offered my very own salon to manage and operate. After praying about it, I invested my savings, got some investors to back me then I took a leap of faith and decided to become an ENTREPRENEUR.

And just like that, I was the Operator of my very own nail salon without much experience. God reveled faith to me through every obstacle I've faced. From learning to trust that He will never Leave me nor forsake me to believing that He has a purpose for my life. It is also through many people that God could restore my soul. He renewed my strength and teaches me daily how to love and be confident in myself.

MY FAITH WALK TODAY

God RENEWS my faith! Sometimes there are days when walking within my purpose becomes difficult and the challenges of being a new business owner becomes overwhelming. There are also times when I'm not spiritually in-tune, I will not pretend to be perfect, but I can say that I am not where I was just 4 years ago, The Lord has strengthened me to endure through seasons that are rough. Life for me has been a process.

A process of renewing my mind to the word of God. A process of learning to love myself for me. A process of release, it has all been a process. I have matured in my prayer life and I am discovering beautiful things about myself daily and if I continue to walk in the light of the Lord I WILL PROSPER!

WORDS OF ENCOURAGEMENT

Above all else guard your heart, for everything you do flows from it: Proverbs 4:23

ABOUT THE AUTHOR

25-year-old, Ashley Kennedy is a native Louisiana; she is a graduate of Pat Goins Beauty school and a Licensed Cosmetologist. She owns and operates, Regal Nail Salon and Spa in Ruston, La She is the youngest and only black woman to own a Regal Nails Franchise. In her spare time, she enjoys reading, writing, and enjoys painting and photography. Her life philosophy is "the flower must grow, although it's planted in stone."

VII.

FINDING FAITH IN A BURDEN & BECOMING A BLESSING!

CHAPTER 10

NO ONE IS PERFECT!

Elizabeth Eddy,

GRAMBLING STATE UNIVERSITY LA., USA

MY FAITH WAS TESTED

17 years of being the perfect Elizabeth. Question is, what happens when your perfect doesn't line up with everyone else's? I didn't plan about life after high school until two weeks before graduation. I randomly made the decision to enlist in the military. The marines were my first choice because my workout partner was a marine. Then my best friend told me that she was enlisting in the navy and I thought the recruiter was very handsome so I changed my mind and decided to go with the navy. However, the night of graduation I decided I no longer wanted to be in the Navy. Lack of focus and faith in myself left me making decisions that were scattered.

College was my first decision, but I choose military because of someone else. Military became an excuse and escape not my purpose. God had already revealed to me that Grambling State University was the college for me, but once again the result of not having a plan and waiting last minute left me rushing. During the summer, God blessed me to do an engineering internship program at La Tech for incoming freshman.

My desire for a social life interfered with my studies. Instead of realizing the struggles that I experienced during the summer, I decided to go to Louisiana Tech University even though God had already revealed to me I was meant to go to Grambling. Nevertheless, while attending Louisiana Tech University I studied chemical Engineering. My first semester at Tech was another warning sign that I was not supposed to be there. At this point you can just call me Jonah, avoiding my assignment. Once again, I allowed my desire for a social life to distract me from my studies and in the end my grades suffered. I was no longer able to attend Louisiana Tech University so I began to work because I gave up on my purpose. Once again without consulting God and choosing my own path I moved out of town to get a better job and focus on rebuilding myself. One month later I was in a car crash that forced me to move right back home.

GOD REVIVED ME AND REVEALED MY FAITH

God helped me realize that sometimes he will allow things to happen to bring us closer to him. God already knew that Grambling State University was the better school for me. His grace and mercy kept me during my disobedience. Hebrews 4:16 Let us therefore come boldly unto the throne of grace, that we may obtain mercy, and find grace to help in time of need. Am I a failure because I had to start over? No. The moment I stepped onto Grambling State University campus I felt like I was home. I put my total faith in God and applied for Grambling State University.

God took me from a place of instability to a mind that is stable and focused on him. Once I put my trust in God he began to open so many doors for me. I walked into admissions and because of my grades they said that I would have to attend BPCC at Grambling before attending the University. God knew that I needed more preparation for what he was about to do in my life. While attending BPCC at Grambling I maintained Grades that kept me on the honor role. More than 5 of my church members were employees at Grambling State University so I could get admitted with no problem.

MY FAITH WALK TODAY

Developing the relationship that I have with God today took preparation, selflessness and dedication. My life was a complete mess before I made the commitment to live for God. The hardest things were getting rid of distractions. A cluttered surrounding creates a cluttered mind. My house, car, education had to become organized so that my friendship with God could be strengthened. When my house was out of order, my mind focused on cleaning it. When my car needed washing my mind became focused on washing it. I would constantly procrastinate in school so I would always be behind on school work.

My mind was so cluttered and focused on making others proud that I put God aside. Isaiah 40:28-31 states "28 Hast thou not known? hast thou not heard, that the everlasting God, the LORD, the Creator of the ends of the earth, fainteth not, neither is weary? there is no searching of his understanding. 29 He giveth power to the faint; and to them that have no might he increaseth strength. 30 Even the youths shall faint and be weary, and the young men shall utterly fall: 31 But they that wait upon the LORD shall renew their strength; they shall mount up with wings as eagles; they shall run, and not be weary; and they shall walk, and not faint." God is now head of my life. John 3:30 He must increase, but I must decrease. To have a good relationship with God I had to become selfless.

My faith increased the more I put my trust in God. I had to humble myself and put God first. Life was not fulfilling when I put my plans of God's plans for my life. Jerimiah 29:11 For I know the thoughts that I think toward you, saith the Lord, thoughts of peace, and not of evil, to give you and expected end. Communication with God is essential. My prayer life is stronger than it ever has been and I'm learning to pray more. Like any relationship lack of communication leads to a lot of misunderstanding. My faith walk today has me committed to the Lord. We are in a committed relationship with no distractions or side pieces. Talking to God is like talking to my favorite person.

My best interest is all that God cares about. Spending quiet time with the Lord allows me to hear him clearly. There are many things that I want to do. Since I am in a relation with God I know that I need to run things by him first because he sees what I cannot see. God knows what I do not know. God feels what I do not feel.

WORDS OF ENCOURAGEMENT

Even in the mist of your storm know that God can and he will. Sometimes it may seem like you are all alone and no one is listening or sees your tears. I know it may seem hard, but do not give up on yourself. God loves you. You are a winner. You are a champion. You can do and be anything you put your mind to. Write down your dreams and put then with God's plans for your life and watch them come to pass. God is a healer and a way maker. Put your faith in him and he will see you through.

ABOUT THE AUTHOR

Elizabeth Eddy is a young woman on fire for God. Passion to serve the Lord and to serve others have built her into the young lady that she is today. Ms. Eddy is a senior double major pursuing her degrees in the fields of Visual Performing Arts and Chemistry with a minor in Marketing. She is an active member of the Student Government Association where she serves as the Senior Class Senator, Floyd L. Sanders Players and STEM Research Journal club. You can follow her on Instagram @ elizabethbreann or twitter @elizabethbrean. Visit her website www.elizabethbreann.com.

CHAPTER 11

GROWING THROUGH
THE PAIN

Linda Ngo, Dallas, TX

MY FAITH WAS TESTED

My Faith was tested throughout my life, from a tragic death of my mother at the age of 3 due to a few bullets shot by my father, to a dysfunctional childhood from that point on. Growing up without stability, love or traditional Family bonding was my normal and I had no idea how a "normal" family was to be defined. I guess what I'm saying is that Faith, Trials and Tribulations happens throughout our lives and for some, daily, but at what point are we willing and able to understand what Faith or even God is?

So, for me, although my life as I reflect now, has been challenging, I can honestly say that I first CHOSE to go to church in 2004 after I gave birth to my 3rd son. I was hitting a pivotal point in my life where everything was just WRONG, from family, relationship issues with my son's father, finances, learning to be a mother and more importantly finding my identity again....my worth, my value, my joy, my smile....my balance. I was beginning to succumb to what my family raised me to feel....

Unworthy...unwanted...ugly...a waste... a mistake who made a bigger mistake by carrying interracial babies rather than college books. So, at the age of 23, I was disowned by a few family members, a mother of 3 boys in yet another unsuccessful relationship, lost, abandoned, stressed, broke and broken.

GOD REVIVED ME & REVEALED MY FAITH

One day as I was driving with my kids, I had the radio on and a Pastor Rickie G. Rush came on a quick segment titled, "What in Hell do you want, when Heaven is all that you need?" I was like, "whoaaaa, is that language allowed in a church?" lol, anyhow, I listened and thought to myself, "this pastor is funny but he's talking to me! Somebody told him what to say to trick me...lol" I never thought much of it, but then a few days later, I happened to be in the car again around the same time and again, Pastor Rush spoke about my drama AGAIN!

I was finding myself laughing out loud, but learning new things about this Church and God thing. Don't get me wrong, my grandmother forced me to attend church EVERY SUNDAY or I was going to Hell and even Sunday school, but as a young girl going to a Catholic church, I was bored and sooooooo not paying attention to these boring people reading out of the bible and still didn't understand that language. All I remembered was sitting, kneeling, sitting, standing, sitting, standing, kneeling, then dry bread and what was supposed to have been juice, but it had to be wine (another lie my granny told...lol), sitting, kneeling then going home...Yup, for 17 years, that's the only thing I gathered about being a Catholic…lots of prayers, lots of rules and lots of bible stuff I didn't care to understand.

One day, after yet another message from Pastor Rush, I called my friend who was a singer in the choir at Pastor Rush's church and asked her about this whole church thing and what was the "proper" protocol to attend and of course the schedule. She told me the church was at least 2 hours long, I was like, "ummmmm, let me think about this some more…" lol, that was my graceful way of saying, "Noooo wayyyy AT LEAST 2 HOURS…nope. I'm good!" lol. So apparently, God was persistent and had Pastor get me ONE last time, BUT, THIS TIME, Pastor Rush came on TV at ALMOST MIDNIGHT!!! Whatttttt???? Doesn't that man ever sleep? Shouldn't he be sleeping or praying privately somewhere?

Reallllly Pastor Rush and or God??? Sooooo, of course I felt it was a confirmation followed by an odd conviction if I didn't go…lol. So, I went to what he called "Monday School" that night and was completely blown away with the style of delivery Pastor Rush had outside his few minutes on the radio and now t.v. I was laughing like I was at a Biblical Comedy Show and before I knew it, between the friendly members and amazing Pastor, the 2 and a HALF hours was up and it felt like maybe 45 minutes. I was so excited that I was now eager to learn about God and within the first time being in that church, I absorbed a TON of new perspective to counteract my "why ME's" and selfishly, it was my "Educated laughter getaway" from the house WITH my boys. From that day forward, my life was changed for the Better… Empowered, Inspired, Motivated and now… Faith- FILLED.

MY FAITH WALK TODAY

"Lord Have Mercy!" Boy, do I understand that phrase now, lol. My Faith Walk today is understood…. I understand now, why I went through all that I went though. My childhood was spent chasing Acceptance, yearning for love and stability, yet, all I received was abuse and 18 different schools before I graduated. I know my full story is to come in my First book, but that too is a part of my Faith Walk.

I now walk with confidence, even when I'm walking through or on fire, because I truly have surrendered my spirit and gained an insight of my Purpose. I know my trials and tribulations were only to build my strength, gain more wisdom and to see through my spiritual eyes rather than human flesh eyes… I realized I was being groomed to be available, dependable and durable for My God's work and will. I understand Life without Purpose isn't truly living nor fulfilling, just more so, existing. I learned to appreciate people whether I agreed with them or not, for I do not know their story, their upbringing, their reasoning, nor do they know mine, so why not try this AMAZING tool called, "Communications" which includes, respect, questions, answers, listening with an open mind, an open heart and maturity enough to agree to disagree and be Perfectly ok with that. That yields Understanding and Compassion, it yields a better perception for now there are more clarity on Life's "whys" for others. So today, I live with a Purpose to mentor, to love, to give back, to educate, to learn, to inspire, to be inspired, to motivate and to be motivated by any and every one God allows me to meet or cross paths. Although, I have my fleshy moments, I have learned and still perfecting how to tolerate or get through negativity. I have learned how to forgive sooner if not instantly because I know that blocks my blessings. My Walk today, consists of Love, Understanding, Patience, Joy and Gratitude.

WORDS OF ENCOURAGEMENT

My words of Encouragement are simple… Don't assume, don't judge, ask so you don't block your blessings. Sometimes, we cast judgement on those we don't know, yet God sent them to deliver your blessings, but because of your assumptions, you blocked your own blessings you prayed for. Remember that your problem is temporary and it's for a bigger purpose than self, remember that Many are Called, but the Chosen Ones made the decision to be available for God, therefore, "To Much is Given, much is Required." Be humbled that God chose You and remember the Power that lies within your Tongue, Your Voice, Your thoughts and Your Heart.

With God's Grace, Favor and Love, I humbly thank you for your Love, Support and Energy, Linda Ngo

ABOUT THE AUTHOR

Linda Ngo is a single mother of 3 boys, a Woman of God, a Philanthropist, a serial Entrepreneur, a Public Speaker with dreams of Empowering Communities and Spreading Love. She believes dreams become reality if only we can support each other rather than wasting energy tearing each other down. She will continue to expand her Business ventures as well as, creating new ways to Inspire and Motivate our Youth though the latest Innovative ways!

VIII.
IN GOD'S IMAGE

CHAPTER 12

(UNSPOKEN FAITH)

Khadija Young LA, USA

MY FAITH WAS TESTED

I was born with no hair and going back into my childhood, hair was my greatest insecurity. I developed this form of insecurity, from the opinion of others. I never knew hair was a problem, until others pointed it out. As a child, my hair was short, and for this reason, I was teased and ridiculed. Most of my accusers were adults, which made it more difficult for me to cope with. I was very sensitive in this area; I don't think people meant to display harsh words, which would affect me mentally as a child. But isn't that where the enemy starts, in your childhood? And what a vulnerable stage childhood is. As an adult, I learned that those people weren't the enemy, but the enemy was at work within those people and me.

The enemy knew my weakness; people didn't know this information, which was so dear to my heart. "For our Struggle is not against flesh and blood, but against the rulers, against the powers, against the world forces of this darkness, against the spiritual forces of wickedness in the heavenly places" (Ephesians 6:12). I was merely a sensitive child who took things to the heart and my hair was my biggest setback. Although, people would joke and say cruel things about my hair I would still hold a humble spirit, never catching an attitude but showing a graceful personality. I was always a quiet person only exposing my true self to certain people.

I can remember taking a ride with my biological father and stopping at a lady's house that hadn't seen me in years due to my relocation, she said "Your hair is so long now; I thought we would have to buy you a green wig; that hurt me. I didn't understand why people was still coming at me after my hair had grew long, making these remarks that I was already haunted by. This led me to be very insecure of my hair even when it had grown a good length.

HOW GOD REVIVED & REVEALED MY FAITH!

My emotional security was off balance and I was prone to accident due to my insecurity. My mother was a great parent, she did everything in her power to satisfy me; she nurtured as a mother should. Taking her time to comb my hair and scheduling appointments with my hair-stylist every two weeks, I would see Nene (Fletcher's wife) of Texas City, TX. And when I wanted my hair braided Tameka or Margie was the ladies that were available to me. I had my resources, and for this, through time my hair grew long. I was still not satisfied with my results; still I was very insecure even with a good length.

I would even have people to praise me of how long my hair had gotten, but the state of mind I had, I would feel horrible about them even mentioning my hair and it all developed in my childhood; I couldn't shake the mental state that was established in my youth.

As I approach high school I spent more time away from home. I got involved in dance, so I did after school activities such as dance. During high school, I really got into my looks, at LaMarque High school I gained popularity, and begin dating a guy much older than I. I was still very insecure of my hair and my best friends knew this. I would wear a wrap style now; wrap it up at night comb down in the morning. I was doing unhealthy stuff to my hair, such as using dyes, because I was so insecure. I was trying to satisfy myself and cope with hurtful memories.

The enemy really worked against me in this area it was like he kept coming at me with this hair thing, but really it developed into a heart thing and that's worse. It was my fifteenth birthday and I had been seeing girls at LaMarque wearing weave and I loved it. So, I told Ebony I wanted some of that, on March 13, 2004 I begin to wear weave, it was my birthday and all my friends was at my house, there were at least eight girls. I can remember this like it was yesterday; Ebony was doing my hair gluing and laying. The outcome was so nice, it was beautiful, and I absolutely loved the extensions. I got use to them they gave me the length that I wanted and the fullness I desired.

I continued to use the weave and glue, until one day I was taking my hair down, which I had done myself, and the track hair was literally stuck to my hair; I was so afraid, the only thing that was on my mind was; when I do get, this out my hair, it will be no more and I had worked so hard to get my hair to the state it was in. I was so right, once I removed the weave; my hair was chopped up and had come out badly. I screamed and I panicked. I was a teen, torn down in my childhood about my hair being short, and now I was back to short uneven hair Instead of going to my mother and hair-stylist, I turned to darkness and hide my true self. I changed drastically; I got so depressed dancing was not in my interest anymore. My mother was having marital problems and her marriage was ending, so she was distracted and never knew I was hiding my loss. I felt alone, and realize that I needed to tell someone, but whom else to turn to but I, the enemy created division in me.

Once we relocated and I got to Arcadia High I was so quiet, because I didn't want to draw attention towards myself. I had just had a traumatizing situation to happen and all I wanted was to keep to myself. The only one person that I shared my situation with at first was my aunt and eventually my family knew my hair had fallen out. My mother and family pressed me to seek help, but I still lived in fear, I was a damaged person. I would go to see doctors for everything else except my hair. And it wasn't nearly bad at that time. I begin to not care, if I could hide my damaged hair I was okay, although; my hair was damaged I still possessed beauty and grace. I lost myself and my sense of identity; this is when the enemy started to hit me hard. By making me forget my problem, I hid from myself. I was blinded by my mistake.

I prayed and asked God to deliver me from hiding myself, it wasn't working anymore, and the devil was on me and creating me into a person that God never intended for me to be. So, I started seeking God, which was the best decision I could have made. I asked God to reveal me and give me liberty.

I begin pressing into him, showing him that I desperately needed him. I wanted answers but all I got in return was emptiness, little did I know God was there the whole time listening to me pray and speak to him. He finally spoke to me and told me in my spirit I hear you. My prayers got answered, I got into a confrontation and I was revealed, through me being revealed, I was revived. It was embarrassing at the time, but it helped me so much. Every person you meet in your life will play a part and some hold major purposes. Never take people for granted, I count every person in my life as a blessing to me. The good and the bad, even my mistakes are a part of me.

WORDS OF ENCOURAGEMENT

I just want to encourage all young women to never be discouraged about what others must say about you. That is not important, what is important is what God says about you. He is the author of your story, not people, people will let you down. God will never leave you or forsake you, and this is true, it is written and God can not lie to you. Had I been covered by the blood of Jesus and knew the word at a young age this might not have happened to me. But this is a spiritual battle field that we are in. And there is no time for games; Satan is at work day and night. I was called out of darkness, out of my destruction, and lead into the light I could have easily strayed away from God, but I didn't because he is my help and he covers me. When trouble comes

I can't look down; there is no time for that, the enemy is waiting for you to drop your head and look down, so that he can steal something precious from you. You must remember that the most powerful place you can be is on your knees praying and fighting in the spirit. I had excessive fear built up in me and I knew this was a major part of my problem. We can't see what's going on in the spiritual, but in the physical we can lift prayers to help us fight in our spiritual life. And we can't afford to live in fear thinking about past and future problems.

I experienced self-hurt and self-abuse towards myself and I was the only one to blame, it was my fault. If I had not listened to the opinion of others I wouldn't have went through such a terrible storm. That is why be careful who you expose your children to, who you let them hang around and associate themselves to. Things can be spoken into existence; witchcraft is at work in the world. And the tongue is powerful; the tongue can bring life or death. Because of my hair loss, I have drawn closer to God my relationship with him is so thick, a bond that cannot be broken, a love that is never ending, and truly a blessing to have him in my life.

I feel for the little girl with insecurities, and I think all girls should know that no matter your hair length, your size, your features, or your color; you should embrace your beauty. God made all of us different; no one in the world is alike. And if everyone in the world were alike the world would be a boring place. No one deserves to feel like they can't be themselves.

ABOUT THE AUTHOR

Khadija Young is a writer, operating at Grambling State University, pursuing a degree in Child Development and Early Literacy. She is from Arcadia, LA. She resides in Grambling, LA.

Khadija enjoys singing praises to God and taking mission trips to foreign places to spread the gospel of Jesus.

She is a full time Christian and lover of Jesus!

Email: KhadijiaYoung@yahoo.com

IX.

SERVING GOD IN FAITH

CHAPTER 13

A PRAYING MOTHER!

First Lady & Evangelist Savoy Nicole Colbert, TX, USA

MY FAITH WAS TESTED

I remember as a young girl, my mother who had been a prayer warrior for over 40 years would pray and intercede for her children and others. She would pray to God to bless her seed. The words of her prayers have sustained me and she would often say, "Lord I give my children back to you". I was reared in the church and I was the daughter of a Pentecostal preacher. My parents were both kingdom builders and reared their children in church and taught all ten of us the fear of God! I often say, if nobody else was at church the preacher's kids would be there!

We went to Sunday School, YPWW, Bible Band, Sunday morning service and every other service in between. When I got in high school, I often say "When I get grown I am not coming to church like this". After I graduated High School, I went away to college.

This is when my downward spiral began. I like to rewind to 18 years' prior, my Mother was giving birth to me and my umbilical cord wrapped around my neck and from what I was told, the Doctor had to do an emergency C-section. Even at birth the enemy was trying to abort my destiny! So, getting back to my college days, I began to date a guy in college that I know was not of God. He was a Father's worst nightmare! I was raised as a Daddy's girls and my 6 brothers were very protective of me! I became very isolated and distant from those close to me!

GOD REVIVED ME & REVEALED MY FAITH!

But my Mother was a praying woman and she often was given insight by the Holy Spirit. She often would tell me when I came home from school that God has a calling on your life and you can't run forever. God had begun to deal with me in dreams and show me that if I continued with this down spiral, something very traumatic would happen. I did not listen and by my 20th birthday, I was involved with a man that had no regard for God and started being abusive verbally and physically. I knew this was not for me, but he would apologize and I would allow him back in my life. He would always be angry with me, because he knew that God had his hand on me as well.

My mother never stopped praying for me and would continue to show me unconditional love. The Bible says, "Train up a child in the way he should go" (KJV, Proverbs). I believe that I knew deep down that being involved with someone that did not even know God, less on attend church was a big mistake. One day we were out of town, this one night he thought I was seeing someone else. He hit me a with his fist in my face, and I began to fight back. I have never told this to my family, but I began to bleed and fear for my life. And I promised God after our last fight that if he allowed me to escape, I would never come back and I did not. Soon after this he went to jail. Many of women have died from domestic violence, but I walked away. I knew that God had called me to a higher place and I couldn't allow this toxic relationship to keep me out of the will of God!

MY FAITH WALK TODAY

I believe in the power of prayer, and I sincerely know that God created me to minster to others through my story. My testimony paves the way for the woman, wife, and mother that I am today! The God I serve can deliver you out of any situation. My Mother is now resting in heaven, but I understand now that "prayers don't die they multiply". We should never underestimate the power of prayer. Women of God don't ever stop praying the power of prayer cannot be denied. Prayer saved my life and birthed me through to my purpose. I am now happily married to a wonderful man, he has been a senior pastor for over 9 years, and we have four children.

He treats me like a queen and I know now why God allowed me to experience such turmoil in my former relationship. I had to go through that to get to this; I would not trade my journey for anything. It had to fall apart so that God could pick up the pieces of my life and allow me to start again. I praise God for another chance to live out my purpose and minister to those that are yet in the thick of it! You can make it! You need to know that you were birthed for purpose.

WORDS OF ENCOURAGEMENT

I would like to encourage each Mother that is experiencing a child that has gone astray! Love is a powerful force, my Mother was strong and stern but at the same time she gave love, and she did not allow my failure to define me! She told me after I came back home that she prayed for God to change my mind towards my ex-boyfriend, and God gave me the strength to walk away! I was birthed for purpose and God allowed me to go through that abuse to help other women.

The Bible says we are "fearfully and wonderfully made". When purpose is involved the road will often be rocky and filled with heartache and headache, but God will turn the situation around for you as, he has done for me!

ABOUT THE AUTHOR

Lady Savoy Colbert accepted Jesus Christ at a young age, and later renewed her passion for Christ, and rededicated her life to Him, after college. She is a native of Dallas, Texas and attended Texas Woman's University in Denton, Texas. She is the tenth child of the Late Supt. A.D. Rylander and Missionary Marion Hawkins Rylander. She served under their leadership at the Greater True Vine Church in many capacities. She married the love of her life Rev. Charles Colbert in 2001. He is the Senior Pastor of the Greater True Vine Church located in Desoto, Texas, and together they have four beautiful children. One of her greatest joys is that of being a Mother to their children. She enjoys reading, traveling and encouraging others to be their "best self". Lady Colbert enjoys mentoring and ministering to young women in crisis as well. She received her Missionary/ Evangelist license in June of 2015 under Texas Northeast 1st Jurisdiction in Dallas, Texas.

She currently serves as the Women's Department President at the Greater True Vine Church in Desoto, TX, and she loves to serve beside her husband in ministry. She is also the Co-Founder of SISTERSACT an Organization that celebrates and facilitates training of women in ministry in all areas. Lady Colbert is currently attending Southwestern Assembly of God University and is in pursuit of her Degree in Human Services, with a specialization in Christian Counseling. She also is a volunteer for the Family Place, "Women against Domestic Violence" and was recognized as First Lady of the year. Lady Colbert also sits on the board of Directors for the "GREATER OUTREACH CENTER".

God has given her a desire for Kingdom building and she desires to please the Lord with all her mind, body, soul and spirit. Lady Colbert believes in the power of prayer and coordinates prayer services weekly at her local church and a 5am weekly prayer conference line. Lady Savoy is dedicated to seeing the WOMEN of GOD empowered and enabled to live a holy and whole life through Jesus Christ.

CHAPTER 14

TABLE FOR A FAMILY OF SIX

Dormeka Pearce, LA, USA

MY FAITH WAS TESTED

In college, I met my husband. It was amazing how the Lord directed my path through his word. A trusted friend in Christ shared with me at a prayer meeting that God wanted me to marry. This caught my attention! Two weeks of pondering on the prophetic word in my heart, I walked into the university's library and met my husband. He always tells me that he knew I was the one that day! After we met God's confirmation was amazing to me! A year later, we were engaged, another year and we were married.

After the wedding, my faith would ultimately begin to be tested. I felt like giving up at times. I would give birth to 4 beautiful children in roughly 4 years. Most people could not recognize that this was a part of God's plan for my family. a Most could not accept that this has been a part of

God's will for my life. A year after I was married we had our daughter, and our 3 sons. Our children were planned and are 16 months apart. While most people believed that I was throwing away my life, all I could see was my future, God blessing future generations for his kingdom.

A lot of people felt like we did not have a plan for our lives. We felt like we did not have much support. It painful to deal with because to us, we were simply doing what God said. We wanted 4 children and it was God's will for our lives.

There was so much going on in our lives at that time, I was diagnosed with post -partum depression Indeed our faith was tested.

GOD REVIVED ME & REVEALED MY FAITH!

God would send encouragers (people that I did not even know) to confirm that we were supposed to have 4 children and even call out the purpose of my children. God did not reveal faith to me in an instant but it was revealed by mostly what I lived through. I had to live his word and walk in his word. Sometimes, you don't know just how much you are not submissive to God until you hit the rough places in life. I wanted to do the Lord's will but at the same time I was concerned about our effect on people. We must be fully submissive to God to receive what He has for us.

God revived my faith by revealing to me that I could trust him no matter what was going on in my life. God doesn't ordain trouble but when trouble comes, God will be sure that it works out for your good. He revealed to me why I had to have children at such an early age and why he had me marry at such an early age. To do something spectacular for God, you must have faith to believe what God said and never doubt it.

He began showing himself mighty in our lives even though no one could see it but us. God delivered me and my husband from some things in our childhood. This was a demonstration of God's power in our lives. God would begin to reveal more about our purpose for our lives through our children. I honestly believe that if we hadn't had our kids, we wouldn't be who we are today. God used our kids to bring out the best in us. We learned to work together as a family. We learned how to love each other unconditionally. God literally revealed to us that his hand was moving in our lives.

MY FAITH WALK TODAY!

Today I can boldly declare that I am not ashamed of the choice that I have made concerning my children. I have learned that God has ordained my marriage and that he has in fact blessed me with 4 beautiful children. They were planned and they were created on purpose and with purpose because God ordained for us to do it. I am less concerned about what others think of me today and more concerned about doing the will of my father. I am dedicated to walking in purpose with my husband and fulfilling all that God has ordained us to do as a family.

What God has ordained in my family will always be first! I often hear stories about how women are so hurt by family and friends talking about the amount of kids they have, but what people do not realize is that they are speaking against their future. You should be proud of any woman that wants to stay home and raise her children to ensure that they get a great start off in life. God has a plan for those babies.

We are a family of 6, a family that is going to shake up the kingdom of darkness and shine forth our lights to the world. The word says that he prepares a table for you in the presence of your enemies. This means that what the devil meant for evil, God will use it for your good. The Lord has even used me to encourage other women to walk in purpose in the home and to not be ashamed of what the Lord ordains for them to do. God is the God I love and the God that I serve and there is not one day that goes by that I am not grateful that I said Yes to God. I am glad to always say, "table for a family of 6!"

WORDS OF ENCOURAGEMENT!

I want to encourage women to nurture their children, love them and point them in the right direction to be all that God has called them to be in the kingdom.

ABOUT THE AUTHOR!

Dormeka Pearce is a Christian writer and has been called to God's ministry. She shares both insight from biblical knowledge and experience. She believes in the word of God as God's final authority. She has a heart for marriages and families and is the co-founder of Purpose in Marriage Ministry under the umbrella of Cornerstone Ministries, which helps to strengthen marriages with the word of God. She has a desire to see the lost saved and come to know Jesus Christ as Lord and savior, she also believes in the supernatural power of God. She also serves with Word of God Ministries.

CHAPTER 15

GOD HAS MADE ME FIRM; GOD HAS MADE ME STRONG

Peta Oates Blake, Jamaica

MY FAITH WAS TESTED

My greatest ambition as a young woman was to be sought after. I wanted to be great; someone that was known worldwide. As such, I worked earnestly at being the best at whatever I did. At age 24, it was prophesied to me that God had greatness in store for me and He wanted to use me for His will. This was my first real encounter with God, although I was brought up in church. God used one of His servants to minister to, encourage and mentor me.

As I grew in my relationship with God I realized that God had a purpose for my life. My ambition to be great was fueled by the passion and will that God had for my life. With this new revelation, my sole purpose was

to serve God. As such, 1 Corinthians 7:34 became my conviction "…
An unmarried woman or virgin is concerned about the Lord's affair:
Her aim is to be devoted to the Lord in both body and Spirit." Serve the
Lord I did. I devoted my life to the local church I was a member of and I
did everything my hands could find to do. Over time I became involved
in all areas of ministry holding positions such as Cell Ministry leader,
Single Ministry Committee Member, Training

After several years, serving in the administrative capacities, I felt a need
for growth. On a personal spiritual level, I was so busy my relationship
with God was almost non-existent. As for, ministry I felt a need to move
from the administrative to impacting the lives of women. I became frustrated with work as I did not think I was fulfilling God's purpose for my
life there either. In addition, I felt the need for a husband, I was lonely,
tired of going home alone and needed someone to share with.

However, I continued to serve in my administrative capacity as I could
not bring myself to tell my Pastor and mentor my true feelings. I com-
forted myself saying there was no one else to take my place thus I couldn't
leave. Attempting to fill this void, I joined the Women's ministry which
only added to my already packed portfolio. Secularly, I was a tardy, miserable complainer doing the bare minimum to get by. The relationships
and activities I engaged in were not appropriate for the Christian walk. I
led a double life. This lifestyle life led to guilt, crying, burn-out, unhappi-
ness and frustration. Most of all I was disobeying God, I knew there was
more that God wanted me, but I was afraid. Afraid of disappointing
others, afraid to step out in faith.

At one point, I tried running away so I had an excuse to leave. I applied
for a course overseas but God would not have it that way. As such, I
had to face my responsibilities head on. While participating in a session
designed to improve the leaders of the church. We were asked to share
with each other some things we saw needed improvement. It was during
this session I was told "my life is not manifesting God's purpose."

This one statement troubled me and was the catalyst for a myriad of changes in my life over the next two years. My first reaction was anger. I could not understand why this was said. I was one of the most active persons in church even though my ministry did not involve preaching, teaching or singing. My next reaction was to pray, asking God for direction. The word from God was "your pulpit is not the church." This led to me blogging in the form of a devotional. The devotionals were designed to inspire, empower and equip women to fulfil their God-given purpose.

It was very clear to me that my purpose on earth is to empower, motivate and inspire others to fulfil their God given potential. As such, I enrolled in a Positive Psychology Masters course. This was to increase ability to help others to thrive. Enrolling in this course as well as working on my first book made me feel alive again. I felt as if I was on the right path to fulfilling God's purpose for my life. I could cope with work and I did what was required of me in ministry – going through the motions. The book was published December 2014 and I was doing very well at school. Positive Psychology became evident in my everyday life and the impact I was having on others.

Thou many readers were being blessed, I felt the calling to move even more. I was discontented, I felt as if I was not being true to my God, to my readers or to myself. I encouraged these persons to full-fill their God-given potential yet I was not fulfilling mine. "Why was it so hard for me to leave this job?" Again, I was afraid, afraid of disappointing others.

I carried the additional burden of living a double life. Hardly anyone knew about my other life where even though I wrote and published a devotional I was sleeping with a married man. Even though I was so devoted to church for eleven years maybe only two years in total I abstained from sex. This I could not share with my family members, my board members and some of my closest friends. I simply lived with the shame and guilt, asking God for forgiveness over and over, fasting, praying, memorizing the fornication scriptures, condemning myself, being involved in church and being the perfect Christian everyone thought I was. This changed nothing.

Knowing that God wanted more from me, I changed my prayers asking God to make a way out. "Lord provide a man that I can be honest with about my past because I am tired of this same old sin. I cannot fulfil the purpose you place on me if I continue this way." A few days later I met this man. Very soon I realized this was God answering my prayers; He did not forsake me. I was being prepared for the next level. I knew that this was the fulfilment of the prophesy that came earlier in the year, that I was to be married by next year. Still I was afraid. Again, I doubted that God was indeed my Salvation.

I consulted with those I usually seek approval and support from which was not forthcoming. This time, I questioned God, I fought, I cried, I was angry, disappointed and frustrated. I became resentful. At times, I remember wishing I could become pregnant to make it easier for me to resign from all church activities, get married and even leave my job. I would have received sympathy, but as it was, those I sought approval from could not understand why I would want to leave my job to start my own business and pursue my studies, resign from my dignified positions in church and in addition get married to a man that was "unequally yoked."

Despite others not understanding or agreeing with the decisions I was making; I knew the purpose God had for my life and what I needed to do to move to the next level. Soon I came to realize that I had to trust God. I had to step out in faith.

GOD REVIVED ME AND REVEALED MY FAITH

"Don't be afraid!" Elisha told him. "For there are more on our side than on theirs!" 2 Kings 6:16

When you feel like no one is with you, God always provide the least likely of persons to support and encourage you. One morning, maybe one of those mornings when I was at home, either working up the energy to go to work or maybe one of those sick days I took from work so regularly I am not sure, but I was still in bed when I received an email from one of my devotional recipients. The email encouraged me to make my decision about what God is telling me to do before it's too late. On that day, I wrote my resignation.

It did not get to HR until a month after since I still wanted approval from the person whose opinion I valued the most. Still frustrated, crying daily and losing all interest in ministry and work, I could not take it any longer. When I met with my school group later in the day, it was evident that something was bothering me, as such the members of my group enquired what was wrong, and after explaining they instructed me to submit the resignation after the meeting was finished. I submitted my resignation and left my job a month later.

The only word I could use to describe how I felt was FREEEEEEEE-DOOOOMMMMMMM. I suddenly felt a peace. Indeed, this was a peace that passed all understanding.

During this time of turmoil my main support and cheerleader was my husband to be. He supported me every step of the way. When I told him about the desire to resign, He suggested a resignation date. I asked him if he was concerned because neither of us would have an income, as he was not working at the time. His response was no, I found out later that he gave me that date because he figured he would be able to provide for both of us by then.

A month after I left my job, my fiancée started his new job in a managerial position. I found the courage to resign my positions at church two months after and I got married a year later.

My business is moving into its second year and I am in my final year of school. I maintain excellent grades and my business is flourishing.

Opportunities are coming every day to impact women with my writing.

This experience taught me that despite us doubting God's plans for our lives and although we look to others instead of Him, He remains true to His word that "all things work together for the good of those who loves Him." He knew my heart, my hopes and my desires and although I was slow to act on His instructions He still worked on the good desires of my heart.

I still have not regretted submitting my resignations, my school fees are always paid, my business and marriage are flourishing. Spiritually I am building a better relationship with God. Regarding, my writing, I have written several motivational speeches that have impacted others, ghost written a best seller devotional that have impacted many lives already and is working on a sequel to the devotional and a book about church women who overcame sexual issues.

MY FAITH WALK TODAY

As a child, my mother taught me to depend on God to provide. We live in Jamaica and I have always heard my mom say "Mi bend mi mine to mi condition". She was saying whatever the circumstances I accept it and I will find a way to make it work.

For a period before I resigned, God had me praying for contentment. Philippians 4:12 says "I know what it is to be in need, and I know what it is to have plenty. I have learned the secret of being content in any and every situation, whether well fed or hungry, whether living in plenty or in want." I believe this period of prayer was in preparation for my current faith walk.

Leaving my job to start a business did not mean that my bills disappeared. It meant that my income would be less for a while and that I would not be earning a steady income. As such my standard of living changed and I had to adjust. In addition, I am newly married which means my circumstances have changed, for e.g., living with someone for the first time since leaving my parents' home and considering someone else when making every decision.

That prayer of contentment that God had me praying prepared me for these changes. It took me to a place of peace, a place where I no longer worry about tomorrow or what others think. It took me to a place where I realize that happiness is my choice, I can either let my situation get me down where I complain or I can choose to trust God and do what is necessary to make me happy. Jeremiah 29:11 encourages me that God has a plan and it is a good plan, a plan to prosper me and not to harm me, a plan of a future and hope. So, I am at peace with God's plans for my life and I choose to be happy.

Most importantly however, I am at that place where God is my salvation. I am no longer afraid of men, now I trust in God. Instead of depending on myself and others for help and approval, I turn to Jehovah who is my salvation and defense.

Secondly, I am learning that my life should be mainly about pleasing God and not others. The Bible tells us about the story of Bathsheba and David, David was afraid of what others would think so he did everything to cover up His sin, forgetting that God saw what He did and He sinned against God. I strongly believed if I had stepped back and focused on my spiritual life, God would have helped me to get over my sexual issues. Instead, I carried on with the work of the church, afraid of how persons would view me. Yes, I sought help but I received comfort instead of counsel. My active participation in church did not prevent sinning continuously.

Today, I am learning to deal with my cobwebs. I have learnt that God wants to help me in every area of my life but I must obey Him. Philippians 2 :12-13 encourages "Wherefore, my beloved, as ye have always obeyed, not as in my presence only, but now much more in my absence, work out your own salvation with fear and trembling." As such my faith walk today is about reverencing God with my life. Instead of ignoring the issues in my life to help everyone else, I will also ensure that I am spiritually, emotionally and physically well.

WORDS OF ENCOURAGEMENT

Many times, instead of following our dreams and aspirations we allow others or circumstances to deter us. This is usually because we are afraid of failing. We are afraid of disappointing ourselves or even those around us.

My encouragement to everyone who reads these words is to trust God. Be sensitive to God's will and purpose and calling on your life. Where is, God telling you to go? Where does he want to move you to? Is there anything in your life that needs to be removed? Is there a higher place that you need to go? Are there people you need to impact?

The Bible encourages us to let God establish our plans. Once you build a relationship with God and allow Him to establish those plans, He will do exactly that. You just must have faith that God will get you through whatever situation will come.

Secondly, believe in yourself and the plans that you make. Believe that you can achieve anything you set your mind to and pursue it with everything you have. People will dissuade you, some out of genuine love and fear, some for envy and some because they just do not understand where you are on your journey. However, if you are being true to you and God go for it.

Thirdly, maintain a positive attitude always. Circumstances will come, failures will come, disappointments will come but these can only stop you if you allow them to. Your perception will determine your success. Therefore, maintain a positive attitude, view them as stepping stones instead of blockers.

Lastly, if you haven't accepted His gift of salvation, consider accepting it today. Trust God today, He will make you firm, He make you strong.

ABOUT THE AUTHOR

Peta Gayle Oates- Blake is an award-winning Author, Positive Psychologist and radio host. She empowers others to find and live their God-given purpose. Armed with the inspiration that her pulpit is not limited to the church she wrote an award-winning devotional, "Every Woman Devotional: The Journey to Becoming a Woman of Purpose." Having grown up in conventional Christianity she also seeks to impact others on her radio program Positively Speaking on www.ufdvgospel. com, through ghost-writing. Founder of Positive Consultancy Ltd, she helps individuals and businesses to thrive. Peta Gayle Oates- Blake can be contacted at 1876 351 1492, positivesolutions2015@outlook.com or Petagayle.oates@gmail.com

CHAPTER 16

FREE FALLING BY FAITH

Pastor Dianne Mcpherson, TX, USA

MY FAITH WAS TESTED

My life is a testament of Faith! It is such an honor and privilege to know that the God I serve and have committed my life to had a purpose of Faith for my life. Never asking for this thing called Faith and it is strangely amusing to me that as a believer the word has been used so loosely and not even recognizing the power that is behind the word Faith. Early in my Christian walk I can remember learning the scripture in Matthew 17:20.

Some years ago, I was in a conversation with a young lady and we were discussing the ups and downs of life and how sometimes, we find ourselves back in the same places that we thought God had delivered us from. In our talk, she told me that I should think of my journey as free falling with Jesus. When you think about the word free, you immediately see yourself being rid of those things, places, people and hurts that have caused you to sometimes spiral out of control or even lose focus and wander away from Jesus Christ. Being free is a gift that only God can give you. I was afraid of heights so the thought of falling did not settle well in my spirit because, I never wanted to be labeled as a failure in anything; there was this need to trust God and allow my faith to prevail over anything else but, there was still that uncertainty of how things would turn out. Free Falling by Faith became more transparent in my life when my family was faced with being homeless for exactly four months this time last year.

GOD REVIVED ME & REVEALED MY FAITH

God revived me during my prayer time with Him. God placed me back in the position during this time to lead and facilitate my FOCUS First on Prayer teleconference line every morning at 6am. This time of devotion and intercession allowed me the opportunity, to take the focus off of my current situation and address the needs of someone else. It was during this time that I felt my spirit being renewed and having that sensation of falling deeper with God and not really concerned with where I would end up, just if it was with him. Free falling became more of a refreshing thought each day. I could really feel that I was in His presence and that when I fell, He was there to catch me before I hit rock bottom. The reading of God's word gave me strength and understanding to what was taking place in our lives now. The journey wasn't about me; it was about the destiny and purpose of my family.

Revived means to restore or bring back to consciousness. The Lord spoke clearly and gave me specific instructions on what the outcome would be and I just needed to trust the process and stand by faith, not wavering at all. I had clearly lost consciousness to my full purpose in Him. The world had beaten me down with routines; its systematic theories of how I should govern myself, that I lost sight of what really mattered. My family is built on the principles and foundation of God's word and every struggle has His stamp of approval on it. When you are called to lead sheep, you will face spiritual warfare, but if you relax and take deep breaths, you will feel the revival that will take place within.

MY FAITH WALK TODAY

My favorite passages in the Bible Are: Psalm 27:1-2; *The Lord is my light and my salvation-whom shall I fear? The Lord is the stronghold of my life of whom shall I be afraid? When the wicked advance against me to devour me, it is my enemies and my foes who will stumble and fall.* Hebrews 11:31; *By faith the walls of Jericho fell, after the army had marched around them for seven days.* These scriptures along with so many others have given me access to the knowledge and wisdom on how I can trust what God is doing in my life. After everything I have conquered over the past 52 years of my life, it is truly by God's grace and power of the Holy Spirit that I live to share my testimony with others. I am secure in knowing that there is divine purpose for my life and it is not just for me, but is for the betterment of those around me.

My faith walk is a representation of the love that God has for me and that no matter what road I travel with Him, I am going to come out victorious! When God allowed me to take my first breath at birth, it was destined for me to live a life of faith. With God, my fears have been demolished, with God, my heart has been healed, with God, my spirit is free and with God, my prayer life is better. After going from one hotel to the next in a period of four months, I finally could see the break-through coming. It was a challenge finding sufficient housing in the area in which I was seeking that would be economical for me. There were several places that would not accept my application because of my past rental history.

In the still of the night, God would speak and reassure me that everything would work out for my good and He would get the Glory out of this. It was the holiday season and my family was in a hotel, but God gave me every resource needed to press forward and still enjoy the time off from work and being with my extended family. I could still prepare my holiday dish that everyone would anticipate receiving, right there in my hotel room. The Lord showed me how to utilize the space and time, to be productive and proactive in my faith. God did not allow us to skip a beat; our lives were flowing as though nothing ever happened. It was an adventure for us, and that's when Faith was revealed to me.

I put my focus on the prize and pressed forward over every obstacle that came my way during this period. Even after being approved and given a date to move in our new place, the time came and then I was told that it would not be ready for another month. I remember clearly God said, that is not the place I have designed for you! Stay the course, do not get weary in well doing, you are too close to give up now. God opened the window of opportunity and we could go to a familiar place where we could be comfortable. It was there, the breakthrough occurred. About three weeks later, we were moving in a new three-bedroom townhome with everything I wanted. He answered our prayers; I just had to wait until what He had designed for me was complete!

Faith has moved me in a place of subconscious intercession for others. Knowing that the Lord is my light and salvation has strengthened me and reassures me of His divine protection and covering over my life. My faith allows me to pray for my enemies, even when I don't have the understanding of their actions. Faith has kept me from being impulsive and trying to handle things in my own way. Faith has given me the patience of Job and the Wisdom of Solomon. Faith has me free falling without care or resistance. Faith allows me the opportunity to trust God when He calls me to intercede and cast out demons, to lay hands on the sick and cover His people with the power of believing, delivering, and transforming prayer. Faith gives me no regrets of the past. Becoming homeless, graced me more faith in God. It prepared me for the dry seasons in my life and it reminds me that if He moved me from one location to experience opportunity in a new location that He will continue to provide. I should put on my safety belt and ride the wings of faith until my work here is done. So, here I am today, displaying my life as an opened book that reads "Free Falling by Faith!"

WORDS OF ENCOURAGEMENT

Strive daily to remain pure in heart, keep yourself as a worthy vessel before God. Your journey will not always be easy but when you trust God through it all, you will stand the test of time and you too can "Free Fall by Faith!" *Trust in the Lord with all your heart and lean not to your own understanding; in all your ways submit to him, and he will make your paths straight.* Proverbs 3:5-6

ABOUT THE AUTHOR

Dianne McPherson, Author of "Touched but Not Healed" A Woman with More Than an Issue of Blood, ordained minister, founder of F.O.C.U.S. Ministry and FOCUS Youth Program in Houston, Texas. She is the mother of three daughters. Dianne is currently working in Education and completing a dual BA in CTE & Biblical Counseling while serving as a spiritual leader-mentor to youth and adults in her community & beyond. Dmcpherson872@gmail.com **https://www.amazon. com/author/diannemcpherson**

X.

COURAGE IN FAITH

CHAPTER 17

HEART TRANSFORMATION

Farah Kal- Remalah, Israel

MY FAITH WAS TESTED

Being raised in a country where people believed that Jesus was beheaded This was my reality but God changed that by the power of his Holy Spirit. I was broken, confused, and treated as a second-class citizen most of my life.

My father was a traditional Muslim in our faith. Our requirements were to follow the guidelines of the Islamic faith. Women in my family wore hijabs. We fasted during Ramadan and followed the rules set by Islamic law. I was taught to stay far away from Christians. Most of my childhood was filled with hate and severe rejection from my father. I was full of hate and had so many issues with the Christian faith. My father wanted a son but my parents had a daughter, this resulted in my rejection. My father moved to the USA to pursue making more money. We would join him there years later because it became dangerous in Jordan due to the daily bombings. When I came to the USA all of what I was taught by my parents was true about Christians.

I would be bullied daily in school. This contributed to my hating Christians and the Christ that they believed in. My heart grew colder towards God. The god that I knew wasn't merciful and I was the same. In the USA I never felt safe or welcomed. I recall a stranger saying, "Thank you for 911." No one could imagine the amount of hurt and shame that I felt, as a child. Then the Lord sent a sweet friend to break up my stone heart. She would consistently sow seeds of faith into my heart to demonstrate the love of Christ.

GOD REVIVED ME & REVEALED MY FAITH

My friend would continue to minister to me by showing me the love of Christ. She never judged me. She even won the heart of my mother through her love for people. She was a light to me when so many Christians were being rude and hateful to me because of my religion. This resulted in me coming to know Jesus Christ as my Lord and savior. After witnessing and experiencing the authentic love of God through my new friend, I came to experience God's love for myself. God opened the eyes of my heart to see, know his love and to witness his goodness. While I could not openly confess my faith to my family. I did confess my faith to my friend. In my culture, if you turn away from the faith of Islam, you are no longer considered to be a part of the family and you are considered an outcast. I must admit that I lacked the courage to openly confess my faith to them because I was still living with them.

My mom did her best to raise me up into the salvation of Allah, which she honestly believed was the way to salvation. She was the first person to ever believe in me and because of how courageous she was, I could make the decision to accept Jesus Christ. She never knew how her love for me affected my life decisions. She never had anything of her own,

I mean not even clothes! I remember asking God, why does she have to ask for help? I wondered those things as a child, I always did but all those things were the bridge to the cross. My mom loved the wrong god, the right way because she was a woman and did not have the authority to stop my father from mistreating us.

One day I received a call from my dad. He never contacted me or even recognized much of my existence. When he called, I knew that it was going to be life changing. During the phone call, he discussed how he was my father and that He would have a right to choose whatever he wanted for me. I planned to go away to college since I just graduated from high school. My dad informed me that he spoke with a friend of his and that this friend wanted to marry me. Now, this may not seem like a bad idea but the man was a Muslim that was 40 plus. After thinking about it, I just simply said ok. I was going to marry a man in a couple of months that I never even met. My father set up an arranged marriage for me.

Well, time went by and we were days away from the marriage date. While I was rocking my baby brother to sleep, I began to seek God and ask God if this was what he wanted me to do. I felt like I knew that I was not supposed to marry this man and that I was supposed to leave my family and home.

I told the Lord that if I was supposed to leave, show me a sign when I open my bible. Mark 10:29- 30 stated, "Jesus said, 'truly I say to you there is no one who had left house or brothers or sisters or mother or father or children or farms, for My sake and for the gospel's sake, but that he will receive a hundred times as much now in the present age, houses and brothers and sisters and mothers and children and farms, along with persecutions; and in the age to come, eternal life." This scripture spoke so loud to me. Not even shortly after that I got a call from my friend saying that the Lord told me that I was supposed to leave. Not having anywhere to stay was very troubling for me. I was scared to leave my family because I did not know where I would live or what I would eat.

My friend then offered me a place to stay until I got on my feet.

Leaving my family would mean that I would not have any legal documents because my father held all our legal documentations like my green card and passport. After getting off the phone with my friend, I left the house with nothing but a purse filled with letters and photographs. I ran as fast as I could because I was scared for my life, but during all the fear present, I knew that I was walking by faith. If my family found me, it would mean that I would literally be beaten and then sold off to a man that was old as my father. God revealed faith to me by showing me that he can deliver me out of all my trouble.

MY FAITH WALK TODAY

After leaving home at such an early age, I was faced with many trials after that. God literally transformed my heart from a cold heart to a warm heart. I am completely sold out for the Lord Jesus Christ and I love what he is doing in my life. I found out that my family moved thousands of miles away, so I now feel safe where I am. I am living in my own apartment and I self-supported. God has been faithful to me through it all and he has even given me a great support system of friends and people that are like family. I found out that my family told my family back home across the sea that I was dead and that I died in a car accident. Although this did hurt me, I realize that God has done extraordinary things in my life and will continue to do extraordinary things in my life. I have an amazing church home in which I serve weekly. Jesus transformed my heart. I am a living witness that salvation is near to all those that call upon Jesus. If you call upon Jesus, he will always come to your rescue. I am proud to proclaim that JESUS IS LORD!

WORD OF ENCOURAGEMENT

Be a light wherever you are. Some people will never read a bible but they may see Jesus in you! Do not walk around with hate in your heart. Love People and Love God

ABOUT THE AUTHOR

Farah Kal is from the middle east. She spent most of her life overseas in Jordan. She loves Jesus. She is dedicated to doing the work of God's kingdom and passionate about seeing the lost come to Christ. She is an excellent photographer and designer. She believes that God can save anyone by the power of the Holy Spirit.

XI.

GOD'S SECOND
CHANCES

CHAPTER 18

"HAVING FAITH THROUGH THE STORM"

Jaimie Cummings, LA, USA

MY FAITH WAS TESTED

It was August 29, 2005, in New Orleans, La. at Baptist Memorial Hospital. My mom was in a hospital bed passed out from all the medication that had been given to her. Oblivious to the fact that there was a category 5 hurricane beating against the windows. Every nurse and doctor was in panic mode, wondering what was going to happen next. My mom's nurse was so nervous she kept bringing my mom medication as if she had never given her any at all. When I noticed that she was coming in so frequent, I had to put a stop to it.

But the nurse didn't care she just went on to another room to do the same thing to another patient. They were trying to overdose patients so it would be less for them to deal with amid the turmoil. Crazy, right? I heard one of the doctors say, "well, she's going to die anyway I might as well kill her." I couldn't believe what I was hearing, but I knew we had to get out of there. By this time the water was already rising and we're surrounded. Surrounded not only by water, but by death. The smell was revolting and the doctors were saying, "let's go, it's time to evacuate the building, patients in one line, visitors in another line." Well, I was a visitor and mom was the patient so that would require us to separate. My mom and I, and another family refused to separate. Because of that, we were kicked out of the hospital without getting our discharge papers, when everyone else did. We didn't know what to do, so we started walking down the stairway. There were people passing out and dying right before our eyes. We thought the same was going to happen to us, but we kept walking. Not knowing whether we were going to live or die. Now that's a test of your faith!

GOD REVIVED ME & REVEALED MY FAITH

Having gone through all those things, my prospective of life has changed drastically. I no longer take life for granted, as if it's going to last forever. Because I was so young when we went through this experience, I was just glad to be safe when it was all over. But now that I'm older I look back and just shout out to God, "Thank You for bringing me out." He has revealed so much to me since then. Yes, God allowed those things to happen to us, but it was what happened for us that got us out. I had no idea that through the storm God had a plan greater than I could see. Not just for me but for my mom as well. At first, all we could see was what we lost, but in reality, we didn't lose a thing. God revived it all and some!

I thought that I would always be the ghetto girl who wouldn't amount to anything, but Katrina came to bring me out! Out of the darkness that had become normal for me. What was meant to take me out brought me out. This experience brought so much together for me. My mom and I were finally able to move into our own home, and I went to college and got a degree. We had been talked down on all our lives so for us this was a second wind. God was revealing to me that we weren't who everyone said we would be. At one time, we couldn't see a thing, but what was overtaking us. God saw beyond what we could and placed us on the right path to get us to where we were supposed to be! He gave me the peace that I needed for us to get through the storm. God revealed that it's not what you go through, it's how you go through it that makes the difference. After the storm my life was revived and revealed to me in a light in which I had never seen.

MY FAITH WALK TODAY

My faith walk today is much better. Thank God for progress. God is my everything. He is my homey. My ride or die. My friend. My front seat rider. Can't nobody tell me that God is not real. He has proven himself to me too much for me to ever deny that. He has the best sense of humor. He makes me laugh, and sometimes mad. He makes me reevaluate myself all the time. Sometimes he shows me things I don't want to see but, need to see. I can't get enough of Him. When I'm weak he shows himself strong to me.

When I feel like I'm on top of the world, He quickly humbles me and shows me I'm nothing but filthy rags. When I feel like I'm not saved, He reminds me of his marvelous grace and auspicious mercy that keeps me day by day. When I feel like I can't go on, He reminds me that He will never leave me nor forsake me. He gives me peace that surpasses all understanding. God constantly reminds me that I'm His precious jewel, rare and irreplaceable. When I'm filled with fear, He reminds me that He's covering me. His presence truly does make the difference. His arms are not too short to reach down and grab me out of anything I'm in. This is the God of my salvation, the light in my path. The one who redeems the 90%. The one who protects me, shelters me, and feeds me. Whatever I need he provides. My steps are ordered by God. He is the love of my life. The one that sends His angels when the enemy comes to steal from me. The one who gave His only son for me. The one who has the power to snatch me out of the fire and not leave a scent. The one who can do miracles so great. This is the God of my faith. The one I live for every day.

My faith walk is not only based on what He's done, but who He is to me. Just because His name is God. Today, I'm in a new place with Him and it's very refreshing. The things God has done for me how can I not trust in Him. Now let's be real, it gets hard as hell sometimes, but that's all a part of the walk. It's not supposed to be all peaches and cream. When reading the bible, and seeing some of the things they went through back then shows me reality. It is proof that it's not always easy. My walk today is a prime example of that. It shows me daily that I must continually have a listening ear to God's voice and be obedient to what He's saying.

The way I just explained how I feel about God, you would think I never get weary. Don't kid yourself, I do. More than just a little bit. This walk is not for chumps. Even when I feel like I want to quit, a still voice inside tells me to keep it moving. My faith today is strong as it's ever been. I have a lot more to trust God for. Now that I'm older with more responsibility and more things coming at me, I must lean solely on Him. With my whole heart. Just to make it plain, I can describe my faith walk as a plant. Most of the time I'm flourishing, but then there are those moments when parts of me wither. The withering is always based upon the atmosphere. If it's not conducive for my growth it withers but then, the holy spirit brings the water that I need to refresh and revive me. The word brings the food I need to grow and stay strong. Jesus is the light that brings the sunshine I need to produce. I just love God and the way He shows me things. My walk is a constant learning experience. Every level I get to there's a vital lesson that is taught in the end. My faith is stronger and because of that it gives me more confidence in God.

Confidence in knowing that there is nothing too big, small, or hard for him to do. I'm believing God for a tree blessing! Which means I must wait longer. In other words, when you are believing for a miracle your blessing will take longer than usual. That is stretching my faith. The more I endure, the more I lean on God. He is able!

WORDS OF ENCOURAGEMENT

If you are weary while doing well, don't faint. God is always there even when you don't feel Him. A Christian walk is just like being in school. Your teacher will teach you all year long, giving you all the information you need to prepare for the next grade. But then there's the qualifier, the test. The teacher gives you all the material you need to study for the test throughout the year, but it's up to you to utilize it. The test is what catapults you to the next level. Let God be the teacher and you be the student. He will teach you through his word and through instruction. It's up to you to do your homework and read. You must study on your own to reach your full potential, so when the test comes you are prepared. The only thing is that when the test comes the teacher is silent. He won't say a word. You must be prepared. God can't lie. So, whatever He said, must come to pass. No matter what's in front of you, behind you, or beside you don't get discouraged. I promise it's worth it more to hold on than to let go. Think about if I had let go when going through Katrina, I wouldn't be here to tell the story. With saying all that I've said the most important part is to never let go of God's hand. Think about how much he loves you. With all the test, you will ever endure, the good thing is that there will be a testimony at the end of it. What's awesome about going through something is that you're going THROUGH. Don't get stuck there. There's an end to your struggle.

CHAPTER 19

MY STORY OF FAITH

Olevia Hall, TX USA

MY FAITH WAS TESTED

Leading by example at all I wasn't a role model to my kids especially my girls I was living a lie so I went back down my dark path I felt deep down it was something I was supposed to be doing in my life God always spoke to me while I slept and it was always clear as what I was to do I had given up on my life the drinking the men, the overeating all of that had a root and until I faced the mirror the devil was going to kill me it wasn't until I went home to wedding that I realized I had to do something about my weight, it wasn't until I realized that the female I was hanging with wasn't really a friend how could I call her that if she seen me engaging in reckless activities and knowing I was meeting men on line and sleeping with them and drinking and driving drunk all the time but said nothing.

I really couldn't hold her at fault because I was grown and my choices was that of my own, at what point do I stop?

It came a moment one day that I was tired of everything I just wanted to die and make all the pain go away so I had to do what I didn't want to do and that was pray I was tired of being the way I was tired of hurting tired of being used and I just needed all the emptiness to go away. The devil was still at me though telling me I didn't need to talk to God I wanted freedom in my life so I lived on the edge and I wanted thrill and excitement. I had to call on the lord I had to get on my knees and pray to Jesus to help me!

1 Corinthians 15:34 "Awake to righteousness, and sin not; for some have not the knowledge of God: I speak this to your shame.

I had to pray and listen to what God was telling me he asked was my life of any value to me?

GOD REVIVED ME & REVEALED MY FAITH

The men that I met online I deactivated the accounts I took the numbers out of my phone see if you take stuff out of sight it is out of mind I learned to value myself more I learned to love myself I learned that God is in me and when I realized that Greater is he that is in that is in the world, that No weapon formed against me Shall prosper, I was taught that sleeping with all those men and letting them have their way was not of God he tells us that our body is not of our own so I had to respect God and myself better so cutting them off and praying over myself was hard because I was always tempted when things seem to get hard for me.

The blood is what save me it was the blood of Jesus that gave my life value it was by his stripes that I am able to live and walk in God's love and by his alone so when I become, tempted or scared I lean not onto my understanding I lean onto God's word and knowing that because he died and arose for our sins that is why I should value my life because God gave his only son for me and my sins so I now live by his word and encourage others that fear is not an option when we have God. We must learn to love ourselves even in the storms and in the darkest moments of our lives we must know that God is with us always in the beginning I asked "What was my life worth"? Now I can say it is Worth everything to me. I now realize all we must do is call on his name "I Love Me", "I Value My Life", I live as if each day might be my last but I know I am free in Jesus.

MY FAITH WALK TODAY

I am so blessed today. I have used all I walked through and survived to speak to women and young girls today. I know I walked through all in my life for a purpose. Some people close the door on their past and pretend it never happened. They hide all their mistakes and secrets away. That is not healthy or what God wants us to do. He wants to turn our messes into our messages. Our test into a testimony. He wants to use us for his Glory! We must allow him to use us. We must surrender!

This is what I have done! I have Surrendered to God. Given him my whole life! All of me. I have given him my dreams, my pains, my battles and my future. And he has done amazing things for me! He has transformed this woman! This woman who was raped, beaten, homeless, and lost. He has used all my past to change lives, help others and save lives! My greatest joy is as a child of God I am redeemed, renewed and revived! I am a Woman of God! And I am using my voice and my story to reach others! To tell them how God can change their lives too.

I am blessed with beautiful grandbabies and a family who love me! I am forever changed and I am forever grateful for all God has done for me. As I look into the mirror I love the woman I have become. I love the life God has provided for me. I know there will be challenges, trials, tribulations, but I also know God fights my battles, provides a way and has a beautiful life planned for me! As Jeremiah 29:11 tells us!

As I am blessed to be an international best-selling author. Sharing my story and all God has done in my life with the world. I pray my story blesses you. That it motivates you, encourages you, changes you! I hope that you see that with God you can do anything!

I am the Founder and Director of an Anti – Bullying Foundation known as HABB (Healing After Being Bullied). It is my mission to stop bullying and to help people heal from the effects of bullying. Bullying occurs in school, work and life. It occurs in children and in adults. It is on my heart to make a difference in this issue. I want to help others to heal, as I have healed.

I live to spread God's word and love worldwide! I know that in this world is in dire need of God's love. As women of God we must speak up and speak out! We must be brave and share our stories and our testimonies. For the sake of our children and all future generations, it is time to take your place and stand up for God!

My personal book is coming out in January! The Dirt I Hid will tell my personal journey. It tells how God saved me, changed me and used me for his Glory! How He turned my life around! How one call out to Him changed everything. I am so grateful for all my blessings! And for the life I now lead! I am excited to see all God has in store for me!

You can be too. My 2017 will be filled with lots of first! And it will be filled with blessings. As God blesses me and allows me to be a blessing to others. I have plans for great things to give back to my community and to help other women! I know if I am obedient to God's will, my plans will come to pass! He will guide me and lead me! He will guard me and keep me safe! As I spread his word and bring people to Christ! I am so blessed to be able to help others and to share my story!

WORDS OF ENCOURAGEMENT

I speak to all women and girls! No matter where you have been or what you have done, you are not too far gone for God to save! You cannot sin too much or done too much wrong to get back to God! Just one cry out or one prayer and He will answer you. He will be there when you call on

Him. He never leaves us or deserts us. He will never forsake us! He will always be in our corner! You can do anything that you decide to be! You can do anything you want if you are willing to work hard for it! Don't let anyone tell you differently! You are beautifully made! You are a child of God! You are amazing! You are capable! You are unique! You are the only you in this world! So, choose to love you!

ABOUT THE AUTHOR

Olevia Henderson Hall was born and raised for the most part of her life in Shreveport, Louisiana. She currently resides in Houston, TX. She is the mother of 7, five daughters and two sons and the grandmother of four.

She recently became a self-published so she adds Author to her bio. She is also a Motivational Speaker and Life Coach & Advocate for Domestic Violence & Sexual Assault Victims. Olevia is Founder of Rebuilt Ministry where her mission is to bring others into the Kingdom under God's teaching.

She is the owner of her own business; Texas Legal Ease where she provides a multi services. God placed a calling in her life to open **(R.A.E) ** Rebuilding After Escaping the new Safe Haven Home opening in fall of 2017. She is a Woman of God who loves giving back who loves encouraging and empowering others as she is a survivor of abuse on all levels yet she is glad her faith in God never wavered.

Olevia is now married to her soulmate William Hall Jr and happy and living under God's commands. Olevia is Founder and Director of an Anti – Bullying Foundation known as HABB (Healing After Being Bullied) Olevia lives to spread God's word and help others.

CHAPTER 20

ADDICTED TO HIS LOVE

Crystal Browder, La, USA

MY FAITH WAS TESTED

My life has been far from a fairytale. I've been through so much in my life that I am surprised that I have lived to tell it. I am a survivor in more than one way. I would not be here to tell my story if it were not for God's love, his power to set me free and to take the taste of addiction out of my mouth. I was addicted to many things that were not good for me before I became addicted to love. However, before I get to that part of my story, I must first tell you how my childhood effected my young adult life. I was a child that was sad most of my childhood for various reasons. I would spend the weekends with my father sometimes.

As a child, I would always have reminded me of what I would never become and that I would never measure up to be. This created in me many emotional issues that would allow others to devalue me as a human. As a young girl, I was sexually abused. For a long time, I was the victim of rape. Due to the misuse of my body, I often felt depressed all the time as a child and wanted to escape the life that I was accustomed to. Sexual abuse makes one numb to their rights as a human. The more abuse I experienced, the more I became numb to how to feel and express emotions. I remember thinking that this is normal, this is the way my life is supposed to be and I just should accept it.

After living most my preteen years with sexual abuse, I finally had my first real boyfriend. He was much older than me and he would be the first man that I loved. Although I was exposed to sex at an early age, I would pretend to be a virgin to cover up the shame of sexual abuse. I had never had consensual sex with anyone before and my boyfriend and I talked about sex on many occasions.

We had determined that we would have sex on one occasion and he had promised to marry me. He was the perfect gentleman and told me about how there would be the shedding of blood the first time that we would engage in sex because I lied and told him I was a virgin. I only lied because I was ashamed to say that I was sexually abused. It is often difficult for someone that has been sexually abused to open and up and tell about their experience.

When we finally did have sex, my boyfriend thought I was lying because I did not bleed and became very angry with me. I tried to explain to him why this didn't happen but he didn't believe me and the relationship eventually ended.

GOD REVIVED ME & REVEALED MY FAITH!

When our relationship was over, I would go on to meet a man that would ultimately help to change the entire course of my life for the next 20 years. At the age of 17, I fell in love with a man that would continuously break my heart for a long time. The brokenness of my childhood never left me, it was as if the enemy was out to haunt me with same issues for a long time. My then boyfriend and later, baby's daddy used drugs, but not just any type of drugs, he used crack, cocaine and other forms of very addictive drugs. Since I was already looking for an escape from sexual abuse and my childhood, I chose to start the use of drugs also. Begging and wanting to be accepted so badly, I turned to him for the love that I needed. His love was not the type of love I was looking for but at least he gave me the attention that I lacked at home.

Within a short amount of time, I would use not only crack but I would begin to shoot up with a needle with liquid drugs. For those of you that do not know, crack is one of the most addictive drugs anyone can be addicted to. My life would take a turn on a dark course in that moment, but looking back I could see where God was keeping me. My then boyfriend would abuse me for the entire course of our relationship. I would have two children during my addiction to drugs that would end up in custody with my mother. During the time of my addiction I would roam the streets looking for my next fix.

I would try to commit suicide on several occasions. On one occasion, I cut down to the bone on my wrist. Sexual assault did not end for me after I left my home as a teen. My boyfriend would prostitute me out for drugs to various men that wanted to have sex. One time, he allowed 10 men to tie me up to a tree and rape me continuously all day. They would beat me and rape me repeatedly until they were tired. After that, I would again try to commit suicide. My addiction would cause me to develop a numbness to life. I would go through the motions of life to not want to feel pain. This was the pattern of my life for roughly 20 years until one day I became addicted to God's love. God literally revealed to me that he had his hand on me by speaking to me through his word and allowing me to feel for the first time in a long time. One day around Christmas time, I realized that my life was not where I wanted it to be.

During that time, I decided I wanted to feel. I wanted to feel compassion for my children and most importantly I wanted to feel God's love. The drugs and the cuts on my wrist were a way to numb the pain that took root in my childhood. I was lost but God came and found me that day when I asked him to help me to love my kids again and to feel again. At that moment, the Lord allowed me to have a compassion for those that I had disappointed many times. He made me addicted to his LOVE.

MY FAITH WALK TODAY!

While in times past I had been addicted to drugs, God took the taste out my mouth and made me addicted to his love. See, addiction is not always bad. It just depends on what you are thirsty after. God made me addicted to Him. I understand addiction very well because I have suffered for many years with a drug addiction. So, when God made me addicted to his love, I understood that I would reap the repercussions of that addiction. His love gripped my heart that night. I was broken but he fixed me! I was depressed but he gave me joy! He restored my relationship with my children, he gave me employment and even gave me a wonderful support system. God did all this because of his love. He has even restored my relational life with a man that I am engaged to be married to. God has restored my life all because of his love. This is what the Love of God through his son Jesus Christ can do for a person, God replaced a drug addiction with a love addiction.

I had faith all along but my faith was not working because I did not know his love. When you get a revelation of his love it will change your life like he did mine. God's love recused me and set me free. Per John 3:16, "For God so loved the world, that he gave his only begotten son, that whosoever believes in him should not perish but have everlasting life." This has held true to me. God's love literally rescued me from my childhood and God has healed me through his son Jesus Christ. Through his son, he has given me everlasting life and it has led me to places that I could not even imagine as a broken child. While my life is not perfect, I am not where I once was and I am not where I want to be, but God is leading me.

I am happy to say that today I have been clean since that day and that the Lord has completely taken the taste and desire for drugs from my life. God's love is never ending and because he loved me, he didn't leave me in that pit of drugs I was in. All I did was receive his love and that gave him the right to deliver me. His love has healed my body and soul, his love has delivered me and his love has restored me! God restored my faith walk in many ways. My faith walk today is growing. I am growing in God and in his word. Although I still need healing in many areas of my life, I realize that I am in his hands and that he loves me. He has been seeing me through many trials and he has been faithful to perform all that I need in my life. He has supplied me with things that I never dreamed he would supply me with. The Lord has allowed me to meet great people that love the Lord and support my family and me. He has a restored my life, rescued me from the hands of the enemy and He has made me ADDICTED TO HIS LOVE!

WORDS OF ENCOURAGEMENT

For those that are suffering with an addiction and that need help in life. I want to encourage you to believe God and to know that you are worth so much more than what you think you are. God loves. You have a purpose! I dare you to try Jesus, although things may seem impossible or things may seem rough, just try Jesus and trust him with your life, and when you do that, I promise you will not be disappointed. God is faithful to see you through every situation and every trial. Have faith and do not give up because weeping may endure for a night but joy comes in the morning. Also, spend as much time with your children as possible and love them if you have them, time flies by! God will fix it, if you let him! Give him it to him and don't take it back! He is always there even if you do not hear him!

ABOUT THE AUTHOR

Crystal Browder is a true woman of faith that has overcome many trials in her lifetime. She is from West Monroe, La. She has lived in various cities across north LA. She has a heart for God's word and to see those that struggle with addictions to know that they are loved and accepted in Jesus Christ. She has a piece of jewelry named after her called, "crystal" that is a handmade bracelet. The bracelet reminds women to, "be the kind of woman to remind women to step up their game." She is the mother of 2, Dylan and Lexie. She is engaged to be married to David.

Email Crystal Browder @ browder813@gmail.com

CHAPTER 21

OUT OF DARKNESS

Brooke Edwards- Arkansas, USA

MY FAITH WAS TESTED

was 5 months pregnant with my daughter and acquired drug charges against me and was now under investigation by the CDI. This was the first time that I ever thought about having to quit in life because I was so scared. God was far from my mind at that time but I knew that If I was going to get out of this situation, I would have to rely on God even though I did not know him. As a woman, I was afraid of leaving my child behind. I spent the first 5 months of my pregnancy incarcerated. This was difficult for me. I then posted bail and got out of jail and went to seek help from my baby's father. When I got out, I learned that he cheated and had another baby that would be born 3 months after my daughter was to be born. It was difficult to express my emotions about how this made me feel but ultimately, I was angry.

We separated for a while after I found out the news and came home and caught the other lady leaving my house. As soon as I was about to leave him for good, I became pregnant with my son and would try to stay but this did not work out. Ultimately, I decided that I was tired of manipulation and that I would rather deal with it myself and learn to be alone. His lies and manipulation did not stop. He married the other lady while we were still together and lied and told me that he did not, no matter what others told me he did. After dealing with all the emotional trauma, I tried to kill myself. After I took the pills and I was throwing up my daughter reached out to me and told me that she loved me. This was the breaking of my life. Her touch would radiate with me until this day. After that day, I decided to seek the help that I needed. I wanted to be free from drug dealing and bad relationships. At this point I would see the course of my life change.

GOD REVIVED ME & REVEALED MY FAITH

In 2009, the drug lord I was working for was arrested and the DTS was investigating all those that worked for him. They came to my house and begin to search through my belongings. After my interaction with the DTS, I became scared and stopped selling dope. I admitted that I had an issue with pills and needed help to overcome my addiction to money. I knew that I needed a higher power to help me stay out of trouble and although I believed in God, I was not sure of his abilities. The night after church I begin to detox from my pill addiction.

Sunday morning, I knew that I was going to church and it would be my first attempt to get the help that I needed. While at church on Sunday the preacher ministered and I knew it was directly for me. At the alter a minister prayed for me and I was completely delivered. This was the first time I would experience salvation. After that day, I was on fire for God and I begin serving. As a single mother, I relied on government assistance for the first time in my life, but after a tragedy in my family, I slipped back into the lifestyle.

My father was out of my life for a while until I got a call from him. He discussed that he wanted to be around my kids and me. One day I received a phone call that my dad was in the hospital and his wife had left him for dead and brother was taking care of him. Not shortly after his battle with cancer, he passed away and we would be left with the choice of burying him in a card board box or giving him proper burial. They were going to bury him in a box and because he did not want to be cremated or embalmed, they had to bury him within 24 hrs. I knew I had to do what I had to do, with a cost estimated with 35,000 dollars, I set out for an entire night to get money.

The next day, I paid 35,000 in cash to the funeral home. The night after this, the Lord gave me a dream. I was praying and I had felt like I was playing with God. I cried out to God and I felt like I had so many things going wrong in my life, I knew that I had to leave that lifestyle for good. I had a dream that I was at my own funeral and it was cloudy and on the side of my casket and I could see my kids and my smallest child's fingers trying to reach for me in the casket. I knew that God was telling me that if I stayed I would die. So, I packed everything in my house and I left. I packed everything and I called my friend in another state and told her I was coming.

MY FAITH WALK TODAY

After leaving, I stayed with my friend and eventually moved into my own place. I don't know how God does it but he does it every single time, he has never disappointed me or let me down when it came to having money. I no longer participate in any street activity. I talk to God like he is my everything. And I have faith that he will always help me. I have church family that have been supportive of me and although my relationships are not perfect, God is mending them.

He works with me every single day and ensures that I am always in good hands. I am an active member of my church and I love the Lord so because he has truly changed my life. God has delivered me from many things, and I am glad I am here to tell my story. God has brought me out in darkness into the light and he has caused me to walk in the light of his word!

WORDS OF ENCOURAGEMENT

If you want something you never had in life, you must do something you have never done. There is no victory without a battle. With God, you always win!

ABOUT THE AUTHOR

Brooke is the mother of 3. She is from Arkansas. As a former drug dealer, Brooke loves to minister to those that are accustomed the street life. She is an active member of her church and is on fire for Jesus. Brooke believes that there is power in sharing her testimony. She loves to hang out with family and friends.

XII

HEALTH

CHAPTER 22

FIBROID LEADS TO
ENLIGHTENMENT!

Lorraine Palmer, London, England

MY FAITH WAS TESTED

Faith: that deep intuitive knowing that you're on the right path.
No fear, no doubt and no second guessing.
Trust in thy "inner self".

As far as I can remember, up until a few years ago, it felt like my
faith was tested daily.

MY MANTRA WAS:

'There has got to be more to life than this?' I would say it to myself almost every day. From an early age, it was the norm to day dream sitting amongst the congregation in Church and think: 'surely this isn't where it starts and stops?' Developing into a young adult brought many encounters with people from different religions, backgrounds, races and cultures which began to expand my knowledge but not my wisdom.

Numerous explanations of the meaning of life, from a multitude of perspectives, none that seemed to fit my 'being'. What did it all mean? Confusion, no commitment, spiraling into food/drink as an escape from the emptiness of a mundane existence (get up, go work, pay bills, party hard, study all night; just to survive). Enter the big 4 0 and it all starts to catch up with me: I felt fat, exercised like a woman on speed and still didn't lose weight, looked like a pregnant woman but obviously was not, with clothes seemingly like they'd all been washed and dried on an extremely hot programmer! Physical body rebellion, mind clouded with processed junk foods and spirit still waiting to be heard. Who knew all this would result in: wheat intolerance, fibroids (non-cancerous growths, one the size of a melon), an early menopause; the test of faith leading to dietary, philosophical and soulful enlightenment.

GOD REVIVED ME & REVEALED MY FAITH

By clearing out my clutter in every conceivable way it was inevitable that I would give myself the best opportunity to tune into my inner self and listen to what God wanted me to know.

Out went things that did not serve me, such as: consuming too much over processed food, people who zapped my energy / who only wanted to share their toxic lives; items I had an unnecessary attachment to and habits that were just a conditioning of my mind (the things I was led to believe were good for me).

In came: me eating more RAW plant based foods and homemade meals - closer to what nature intended; new people who I just had a different kind of conversation with - more spiritual, deep and elevating, based on wanting to know the holy truth (I'm still becoming more aware of this). Who knew that cleaning up my act would lead to a lighter and more enlightened me.

Faith was revived in me as a direct consequence of eating more natural plant based foods, becoming less stressed, decluttering my mind, having less toxins in my body and practicing fewer non-serving habits. Being less externally distracted presented a profound opportunity to journey to the depths of my inner self. Discovering a different way of eating brought harmony to mind, body and spirit, even improving my perceptual set which became attuned to receiving health and wellbeing information galore; inspiring the publication of 'RAW Food in a Flash' - sharing with other women simple steps to a smooth menopause transition.

The gift of fibroids leading to hysterectomy and suffering from numerous menopause symptoms, brought me to investigate a healthier way to be. This wakeup call propelled me into a physical, mental and spiritual detox, reminding me that there IS more to life than this - I was finally able to hear God through my daily meditations and intuition. Once you get rid of the noise, baggage, toxicity, stressors etc. you will hear the answers to your questions. They are always within. Be still. Listen. Connect.

MY FAITH WALK TODAY!

Living on a higher vibration, being more in tune with what is going on within and around me - I am in flow right now. Self-awareness heightened, obstacles diminished, conscious in thought, word and deed. Life is not to be taken too seriously. Having experienced what is beyond this physical life I no longer doubt like that young girl of yesteryears.

It has taken a while to get where I am today. This example illustrates a journey that has endured many setbacks to my highest good:

I visited a place called 'Arbor Low', a few years ago, it is a prehistoric monument and likened to 'Stonehenge' due to its stone circle. Whilst looking around, as you do, I came across some lambs (I was not vegan at that time). I was thinking how cute they looked, their little stubby tails waved so quickly, 'AAWWH they are so cute, they deserve to live a full life and not have it cut short just so I get to eat their flesh'. A few months passed and guess what? Yes, I went out for dinner and ordered the lamb. I had mixed feelings - guilt, shame, enjoyment and satisfaction not necessarily in that order.

Sometime later it became apparent that I was being supported to change my habits for the better. Finally committing to being fully compassionate towards all living beings. The truth is I adopted a vegan lifestyle for health, ethical and spiritual reasons.

Today I: Trust that whatever comes is for my highest good. Destiny is God's will and is already written.

- Go with the flow of life and act intuitively when opportunities present themselves.

- Apply discernment.

- Engage less in worldly activities and spend more time looking inwards because that's where the answers are, right?

- Meditate daily to connect with God. (Meditate first so the rest of the day is in order).

- Am not afraid to die.

- Eat lighter, brighter and higher vibrational foods.

- Laugh every day and get the serotonin pumping.

- Practice gratitude daily.

WORDS OF ENCOURAGEMENT

Give yourself the best conditions for receiving divine guidance. How do you expect to gain clarity if you are constantly distracted? Don't give up if you truly want to experience change for the betterment of yourself, others and mankind. Remember that you have nurtured an array of habits for so long so sustained change/s will not happen overnight. Be compassionate to yourself first and then you can be likewise to other living beings, it will come to you. Trust that things will come at the right time for you and know there is no need to feel left out.

The 'Arbor Low' example can apply to many people, if it has resonated with you stay with these thoughts and see where it leads you. You may have some insights for what you want to do next.

Doable actions to elevate yourself

- Eat fresh food - vegetables, fruit, seeds and nuts are some of my favorites, ensure to eat your biggest meal at lunch time.

- Be kind to others particularly those you don't feel like you want to be.

- Keep hydrated - we are made up of 70% plus water, it is what we are physically.

- Exercise - movement is good for your mental health and general wellbeing.

- Practice stillness - relax or have a bath.

- Participate in a daily practice - meditation, prayer, yoga, mind-fullness techniques or recite affirmations.

- Connect with nature - get outside and step away from technology.

- Take responsibility - you have the answers within.

ABOUT THE AUTHOR

Lorraine Palmer greeted earlier than expected, the menopause, like a hot flash monsoon. It led her on a quest to disable her own menopause symptoms. Today she is a bestselling co-author, RAW Food teacher, Mentor and Chef who specializes in teaching women how raw plant based foods can transform their health. She is currently writing her own book to support other women in similar circumstances.

Contact details

Email: lorraine@uncoveredltd.com

Twitter: https://twitter.com/uncoveredltd

Facebook: https://www.facebook.com/uncoveredltdcom

Website: www.uncoveredltd.com

Pre order her book now @ http://uncoveredltd.com/raw-food-in-a-flash-order-it-now/

CHAPTER 23

YES, JESUS LOVES ME & YOU!

Kimberly Holiday-Coleman

WA, USA

MY FAITH WAS TESTED

As a young child growing up in Texas, I was raised in the church. Some of my most vivid memories of church from that time include being in children's church and singing, "Yes, Jesus Loves Me' and "Jesus Loves the Little Children." The church elders taught us to pray for anything and everything that our heart desired and for any problems we had.

And pray is what I was doing up until the age of nine, when I was sodomized by three neighborhood kids behind their house. I can still recall the chipped green and yellow siding on their house, feel the sun on my face, and the pain of my small body being repeatedly violated while they pushed my face into the dirt and concrete. I remember the confusion, pain, humiliation and shame that struck me in that life-defining moment.

Afterward, I walked back across the street to my home sadly aware, that I was no longer the same person that had crossed the street to play just a short time before. However, long before that horrific event ever occurred, I was already being abused physically, verbally and mentally, at an early age by my parents.

During the same year of my violation, I attempted to commit suicide, my eyesight worsened, suffered chronic hives and both, my hope and faith were lost. I felt worthless and unlovable because both, my earthly father and mother and God seemed to have no use for me in this earthly realm. Repeatedly, I felt my prayers went unanswered, my cries went unheard and the pain was mine to bear alone. I figured that since I was not good enough for God or my parents to love me, I shut down and attempted to become invisible to the world. I stopped singing those beautiful songs. My heart was broken and my spirit was dead.

My young mind could not comprehend why the Big God in the sky would continually ignore my pleas, my cries and my pain. One night, I remember waking up and seeing a long and glowing figure in bed lying next to me. I was frightened then my fear left and I recognized just who and what this apparition was. It was God, lying next to me. However, I would not come to understand why God chose to reveal himself to me until a few decades later. However, I could not comprehend the love of God, only the harsh and relentless pain of man.

Shortly after my 17th birthday, I was raped and impregnated by my long-time abuser. Prior to this traumatic event, I had been routinely sexually molested for years. My abuser insisted that I hide the pregnancy and I did, under the constant threat of physical harm to both, me and my unborn child. Although, I desperately wanted to keep my child borne out of pain and torment, I feared the much greater threat of her becoming a target of this same abuse and worse. I desired a better life for her than I had or could give her, so I made the best decision I could at 17 and put her up for adoption.

GOD REVIVED ME & REVEALED MY FAITH!

After years of being in an emotionally and verbally abusive relationship, I found the courage to leave, after which I chose to enroll in an intensive self-help seminar program that catapulted my healing into overdrive. After completing my first workshop, I met my soon-to-be husband of 17 years. After a month of us being together, he proposed marriage to me and I accepted, but requested he join me in this work because I was crystal clear that I did not want to create the same result with him. So, together, we completed all the workshops offered that year and were married only a year after we met.

We proceeded to have 3 more children together. Two years after the birth of our 1st daughter, we moved to Oregon where we gave birth to our 2nd daughter. Prior to her birth, I had three successful home births. However, things would be very different with her birth. During her labor, we had been playing gospel music in the background and Smokie Norful's "I Need You Now" began to play as chaos quickly consumed us. Our 11-pound daughter was initially born, not breathing. That frightening moment would take place in the middle of our living room, while we were accompanied by 3 midwives and our then, two-year-old daughter sleeping peacefully nearby on the couch.

Our baby daughter was born with an Apgar of 0. The midwives began working tirelessly to revive her lifeless grey body. The tears and grief began to consume me as I looked at her still body from across the room, I began to lose hope and my will to live. My husband immediately left the room and went into a nearby room, where he dropped to his knees and began to pray. He prayed for the life of our daughter and myself. Meanwhile, she still had not taken her 1st breath for about 15 minutes, but it felt like a lifetime.

Upon his immediate return to the living room, our daughter drew her first breath. The midwives grew optimistic and we all cheered and cried. But, they warned that she would probably have mental and physical challenges because she was deprived of oxygen for such a long period. They told us that she would have to be emergency transported to the NICU and in the end, she remained home with us. On that day, we witnessed a true miracle of God. Our daughter, Victoria is a healthy and active child with no signs of the trauma she endured the day of her birth.

MY FAITH WALK TODAY!

A glorious miracle that God bestowed upon me was the return of my 1st child that I had given up for adoption 25 years earlier. All the years that I cried, worried, wondered and mourned the loss of my first born, she finally returned. And while our relationship is a complicated work in progress, I was recently able to witness her marriage and meet her 3 beautiful sons. God also reconnected me to my two older sons that I had gone seven years without seeing due to never-ending conflict with their father. My sons and I are currently rebuilding our relationships with great success.

After my husband and I graduated from college, we returned to the Pacific Northwest. Shortly after moving, I was diagnosed with Stage 2 Rectal Cancer in 2015. Upon completing my 1st round of six weeks' chemotherapy and 33 radiation treatments, I experienced a life-threatening bowel perforation and obstruction which required emergency surgery and I was in the hospital for 10 life altering days. After a couple of days in the hospital, my surgeon came in and informed me that if my children had not been home with me that day, I surely, would have died.

During my time in the hospital, God infused me with the strength to call my childhood abuser and demand an apology for the abuse that I had suffered. By the Grace of God, he did and I was freed! I also, spoke with my Mother for the 1st time in years. Sadly, while I was on my 2nd round of chemo, my Mother died. Once again, the feelings of being unloved and abandoned crept back in after learning she chose to disown me in her will. A few months after my Mother's passing, I was able to talk with my Aunt and she was able to relay my Mother's love for me which was a huge healing for me and for the 1st time in decades, I felt loved by my parents. I was able to understand they had their own issues and story, so I was able to work through this and forgive by His grace.

WORDS OF ENCOURAGEMENT

I have come to understand the meaning of the vision I had during my childhood. It was God showing me He was, and will always by my side and He will never leave me or forsake me. What a powerful and healing revelation for me to discover that God has continuously opened the windows of Heaven and poured out His blessings even during my pain and trauma. At my one year post surgery checkup, they found the cancer is gone. I know that by His stripes, I am healed! I am released! I am loved! I am worthy! I am Victorious!

ABOUT THE AUTHOR

Kimberly Holiday-Coleman is an author, public speaker, mentor, technology blogger/vlogger, community service volunteer, and Wife of 17 years, Mom of six awesome children and cancer fighter/survivor. Kimberly is a University of Houston alumna, travel enthusiast, UH Honors College alumna and Former National Board President of Sigma Phi Omega, Inc. Sorority. Kimberly has also done extensive volunteer work with various Domestic Violence agencies. She aspires to help young children and women who have experienced abuse, find their voice, strengths and passions.

XIII.

HEALING

CHAPTER 24

TEST AND TRAILS PRODUCE GENUINE FAITH

Jeralyn Sims, La- United States

MY FAITH WAS TESTED!

I was raised in a single parent home by a very strong mother who worked very hard to ensure that I had all my heart's desires. Growing up I was showered with love and support from uncles, aunts, godparents, cousins, friends and extended family. Although I was very appreciative of that love, none of that could fill the void of the love, attention, guidance, and support that I desired to receive from my biological father. A father is the first man that a little girl falls in love with and sets the tone on how she expects to be treated by any man. He is her first protector, provider and the foundation of his daughter's confidence and self-esteem.

I lacked that foundation and did not realize the impact my father's absence had on my development until later in life. Everyone around me had high expectations of me and thus I buried my true feelings while I appeared to be perfect on the outside. Multiple issues surfaced as a teen but I was unaware that they were issues. I was insecure and had low self-esteem. I excelled in school academically and socially, but secretly I was struggling with so many issues.

This struggle continued into young adulthood, while in college I became promiscuous, continued to look for love in all the wrong places, and did what I had to do to numb the pain of not having a father. I partied, smoked, drank and took on this invincible persona but secretly I was dying on the inside. I attracted associates that I thought were friends and had a series of bad relationships. One of those relationships produced an unexpected pregnancy. The father did not want the child and I had an abortion. I was afraid, did not want to disappoint anyone and I made a selfish life altering decision. After the abortion, I knew I needed to change and I did the only thing I knew to do, I ran to church looking for help!

GOD REVIVED ME AND REVEALED MY FAITH!

My relationship with God was through others revelation of Him, so this was my first attempt as an adult building a relationship with the Lord on my own. For a while things were going great and I was chasing after the Lord! As I chased after God, I chased myself right into a very ungodly relationship. I was in a situation where I was being controlled, manipulated, abused and had completely lost myself and my identity. I found myself, now a minister in training, in a horrible relationship and pregnant again. Once again, the person did not want me to have the child. After the abortion, I fell into very deep depression. I was on an emotional roller coaster, I became suicidal and I attempted to take my own life on more than one occasion. I gave away the opportunity to experience true love and the enemy began to convince me that because of those decisions I did not deserve to experience motherhood. I felt worthless, undeserving of true love, used, and abused.

With the help of a close cousin and a very special woman of God who prayed for me, encouraged me and she showed me that I could have a happy ending, I left the situation and trusted God as I began to travel down the path of healing. Learning how to forgive yourself is one of the hardest things a person can do and I had to go to the root of my problem, deal with my issues and accept responsibility for my own actions. No longer was I going to be the little girl that grew into a young woman with "daddy issues". I learned how to be myself and began to see myself the way the Lord sees me. I gave myself time to fall in love with myself again.

MY FAITH WALK TODAY

Against all odds, I graduated from college with a BA in Political Science and a Master's in Public Administration. I wear many hats now and one of the most important hats I wear is being a wife. I once asked myself the question, "Will anyone ever love me?" I have a husband that goes above and beyond every day to show me that the answer to that question is yes. We both are two imperfect people who were willing to look pass each other's flaws and see the best in one another.

My husband is the father to two beautiful children and even though I have yet to have my own children, I have still been blessed with motherhood. Of course, the enemy attacked my mind in the beginning. I questioned whether I would have my own children, or if I would have to settle with being a step-mother. But I thank God for surrounding me with strong prayer warriors. My children are in heaven with the Lord. My sins have been forgiven and Jesus paid the price for them on the cross. I now walk in the freedom of God's forgiveness. The grace and mercy of the Lord allows me to be deserving of ALL the blessings that the Lord has for me and especially the blessing of becoming a mother.

I prefer the term "bonus mom" because my desire is not to take the place of my husband's children's moms. That would be impossible because the Lord has already gifted them with loving biological mothers. God has a way of working all things together for our good. I take my "bonus mother" experience as a crash course on what I must look forward to once I am blessed with my own children.

Per Romans 11:29, "the gifts and calling of God are without repentance". I stepped away from ministry completely because personally I felt that I needed to allow the Lord to work on me. There must be a spirit of excellence when you are doing the work of the Lord because it is not about you but about the betterment of the Kingdom. There is a purpose behind everything I have gone through and my prayer is that God continues to use me any way he chooses to magnify his holy name, glorify his kingdom, and bless his people.

WORDS OF ENCOURAGMENT

A wise woman of God once told me to stand in my truth and heal. Everyone encounters their fair share of trials and tribulations in their lifetime, but many of them do not share their stories with others. Things such as fear, judgment, gossip and many other vices of the enemy can be hindrances to transparency in the Body of Christ. My prayer is that my transparency on some of these "taboo" issues can be a catalyst for change. God is waiting on you, all you must do is submit, and turn it all over to him. Stand in your truth, heal and walk in the freedom of the Lord. Never be ashamed of your past but use it as the evidence of the greatness of God. I will leave you with these scriptures, "These trails will show that your faith is genuine. It is being tested as fire tests and purifies gold," 1 Peter 1:7 and "Many are the afflictions of the righteous, but the Lord delivers him out of them all," Psalm 34:19. God bless you!

ABOUT THE AUTHOR

Jeralyn Sims is a woman of God, wife, and a bonus mom to two beautiful children. Jeralyn loves reading, writing, traveling, fashion and spending time with her friends and family. A graduate of Grambling

State University, she is a member of Alpha Kappa Alpha Sorority, Inc. and has a BA in Political Science and an MPA. She works in the mental health field and is the owner of JShondrelle, LLC (www.jshondrelle. com). JShondrelle's motto is "The Exemplification of Style and Grace." Through JShondrelle, Jeralyn provides customers with high end pieces through her online boutique; as well as styling and personal shopping services.

CHAPTER 25

MY STORY OF SURVIVAL

Nicole Taylor, TX, USA

MY FAITH WAS TESTED

It is important to know that I grew up without a father. I had a great stepfather, but I never had a man telling me how beautiful I was. No man ever told me I was loved, and this made me feel unlovable. When I was 27 years old, I met a man. He was my prince charming. He told me everything I wanted to hear. I fell in love… I did not realize he was the wrong man.

Day by day he changed. He manipulated me and my children. He cut us off from family and friends. It got to the point that it was just us. Everyone I'd had in my life had gone on without me. I was stuck. One Christmas night, my faith was tested. I came to the point that I had to make a life or death decision. I was told to be home from my Mother's by 8pm, but I did not come home until 11pm. He was livid. He had a party he was wanting to go out to, and I made him late. He beat me. Brutally.

The kids were crying. He went to tend to them and I ran! I could get out with my phone, so I called my sister for help. As I attempted to escape, he took the car and looked for me. He almost caught me at one point, but a car blocked him. I ran and hid in the woods. With every light, I saw I was sure it was him. I was not afraid of snakes, animals or rodents in the darkness; I was afraid for my life. I was bleeding, had a broken nose, black eye, swollen face, busted lips and a broken finger, I was 7 months pregnant.

In that moment, I did the only thing I could do. I prayed. I prayed for God to protect me and my children. Suddenly, I heard the police on the bull horn and saw the police lights flashing. They were looking for me. He had stolen my car to escape and they let him go.

GOD REVIVED ME & REVEALED MY FAITH

That Christmas night, God saved me. I was lost and did not know how to pray, I did not know what to say. All I knew was that I could no longer walk this journey alone. So, I cried out to him and he answered. I felt a blanket of comfort come over. I knew it was going to be okay. I knew God was there with me.

I began going to church. I felt comfort in God, and I knew there was comfort and power in Jesus Name. I knew that with Him by my side I would never be alone again. He would never leave me or forsake me. He was always just one cry away.

When I would have my weak moments, he would send someone to uplift me with words of encouragement. I remember going to church many Sundays and feeling the presence of God. I felt peace in going, and before I knew it I was giving my life to Christ and my battles to God. He is a healer. I was at my lowest and he changed mine and my kids' lives forever. When I thought, there was no way out, He showed me the way.

MY FAITH WALK TODAY

God gave me that journey to walk through so that I could help others in similar situations. My experience gave me the vision and desire to help other domestic violence survivors. I created V.O.W. Vision Opportunity and Works. We have programs for women and children whose lives have been impacted by domestic abuse.

I almost lost my life. I had a gun to my head but it jammed. CPS came after my children due to my relationship with my abuser. I was devastated and beaten down. My children were too. Not literally beaten down, but domestic violence effects the entire family, not just the one being abused. My children have lasting effects from the things I endured. So, that is why I chose to make a difference and share my story. I thought all was lost and done. But I was wrong. God turned all of that into my message and my testimony. I was so naïve at the time. I thought he loved me but I did not know what love was. I now do! I know love does not hurt you, degrade you, mistreat you, or isolate you! It is my prayer that every woman and girl hear this message and learn from my story!

These experiences prepared me for my work now. God walked me through it. He saved me that night, and I knew it. His love, grace and forgiveness gave me another chance at life. A chance to change the world. A chance to be the reason someone else leaves. A chance to be a voice for the voiceless.

No matter what my abuser tried - and he did try to destroy me and my family - God was there. As I grew in church and in my faith, walk, so did my confidence and my love for God. I knew He had great plans for me and my children. It's not always easy but it is always worth it.

I speak to women who have walked, or are walking in my shoes. I help them and their families overcome. I am an example and testimony to what God can do! I know I am making a difference in this world. My mission is to speak up and help others to know they can do the same.

That night when I cried out and prayed to God changed everything. He can do the same for you. When we surrender to God, everything changes. He is waiting on us to call out to him. So, don't wait.

WORDS OF ENCOURAGEMENT

You may be discouraged and you may be trying to hide the fact that you are struggling inside. You are not alone. The truth is domestic violence does not discriminate. It is found in the homes of the rich and the poor. It doesn't care about race or gender. Make a V.O.W. to change. Surround yourself with positive people that can uplift and encourage you to change. Know that beauty lives within you. You are beautiful. You are beautiful. You are beautiful. Tell yourself this daily. You are worthy of being loved. Love doesn't hurt. Don't settle for an "I'm sorry". You cannot change him! Stop giving your power away. Take it back.

You are powerful and deserving of happiness. Speak up and ask for help! I know you may be discouraged but you must trust the process. Speak your desire to change in your life. It's okay to ask for help. Seek your self-worth. Learn what you are deserving of and accept nothing less.

If you find that you become overwhelmed always remember Jeremiah 29:11 "For I know the plans I have for you, "declares the Lord, "plans to prosper you and not to harm you, plans to give you hope and a future." Today is the day of change, reclaim your life. Redefine yourself and start the healing process. You must choose to be happy. I thank God for deliverance and I thank him for keeping me.

ABOUT THE AUTHOR

Nicole Taylor has spent years motivating and inspiring women to get out of their comfort zone and ask for help. She is the founder of Vision Opportunity and Work (The V.O.W. program) a nonprofit organization that focuses on helping victims and survivors of domestic violence reclaim their lives.

She is a domestic violence advocate, a motivational speaker and mentor to domestic violence abuse victims. With her fun and engaging personality, Nicole connects with her audiences because she was once a victim of domestic violence. She helps others identify the signs of toxic relationships and find their self-worth. Nicole is a graduate of University of Houston Downtown. She received her bachelor of Psychology in 2013 and is currently in graduate school at University of Houston. Nicole resides in Houston, Texas and is a mother of 3. Her famous statement is: nothing changes if nothing changes. After any tragedy ask yourself "Do I want to survive or do I want to thrive?" If you know someone who may need help don't put it off until tomorrow. Tomorrow is not guaranteed. Make a V.O.W. to break the silence. Please feel free to email visionopportunityandwork@gmail.com or you can access our organization at myvownow.org.

CHAPTER 26

FORGIVENESS DURING TRAGEDY

Kirstie Horton- LA, USA

"speak up for those who have no voice, for the justice of all who are dispossessed."
Proverbs 31:8

MY FAITH WAS TESTED

As a child, I can recall close family relationships and visits to grandma's house. There was a lot of small town love and we gathered as a family for prayer meetings often. My mom was a minister of the gospel. I grew up in a protected environment. We could say our mom was loving "strict". She made sure we were never in harm's way. So how could there be something so "off" in the fabric of my family? On the surface, we seemed to have it figured out. I was shattered by a secret of rape that I held for most of my childhood. I struggled deeply with self-esteem issues, eating disorders, depression and suicidal thoughts. Later I would come to struggle with pornography. Rape had left its residue behind and the result was a life filled with fear, shame and heartache.

At 9 years- old, my childhood was stripped from me. I was left with trusted aunts when my mom made a run to grocery shop. I can still recall, I sat eating a bowl of cereal. Quickly, I found myself in the apartment alone. Which was not a scary thought for me. The other kids ran outside to play and I was stuck inside with a headache. I finished up my cereal, put my bowl away and went to the bathroom. Little did I know my young life would change. How I would come to view the world, men, my safety and love, would all drastically change.

There was an older male cousin in my aunt's apartment that day. I trusted him but within seconds I was lead to a bedroom and told to lay down as he forced himself on top of me. The words that would come to ring in my head for years "if you tell anyone this happened you will get in lots of trouble." I was shaking and terrified. I was led to the bathroom and he was gone sooner than I could look behind me. In the bathroom, I wiped, saw blood and was even more terrified, shook and threw up from being nervous. I was not even sure what to call what happened to me. From that moment on, I never said a word to anyone but my brother. He always knew why I was broken.

When I was 15 years old my mom finally found out. She tried to provide a safe place for us to come and tell her anything. I never felt like I could do that as a child and the other part of me was afraid of what this cousin would do to me and what everyone would say about me. I felt like nothing! As a teen, I would hide my food under the bed and not eat or throw up. I liked the feeling of being constantly empty. I felt like I was literally purging myself of hurt and shame and never had an appetite.

My family had no idea of my secret battles and attempts of suicide. Once this secret was finally out, I didn't feel any safer. Calls from family members who did not believe this happened to me would haunt me for years. The older cousin was such a star in school, many asked the question of "what would he want with a child?" To me family was supposed to protect me. To cope, I learned to hide behind walls. I learned to build emotional walls to never be truly known by people. I learned to never take a risk and let anyone in. If the enemy can isolate you, he can destroy you.

GOD REVIVED ME & REVEALED MY FAITH

Rape is hidden into many families. Everyone knows it's happening but the silence is what stands bold in the room. Growing up admitting that you had a problem and needed counseling was wrong. You never processed your pain. We were so caught up in our "religion", we did not even realize that religion and relationship with God was not the same. I was always told to suck it up or when I would finally bring myself to tell someone sexual abuse was a part of my past, they would say it happened to me too as if it were no big deal. I felt that the person speaking these words had become so disconnected that they were living a lie. In my heart, I saw something so broken in so many women who carried this secret. They were not fine; they were not thriving and they were not living lives of freedom. Be quiet they said. Be silent, because silence is strength.

I held this hurt for years and I finally realized this is larger than I can handle on my own. As a child, this was engrained into my psyche. Unknowingly, I had learned that I had no voice. I had been taught that I was small and sharing my experiences with people was a for sure sign of weakness. My whole life I lived in the shadows. The moment I found myself gaining a bit of self-confidence and freedom I would soon after feel the shame of my past. It literally haunted every decision I made in life. I would often wonder if it's obvious that I am broken. I had really hoped they could not see the real me. The me that believed, I was not worthy of happiness, marriage or children. Surely if any man would know the past I carried he would run for the hills. I told myself I was "damaged goods". Christ gave everything to us, that we may know freedom. God is holy; therefore, he cannot allow sin to go unpunished. This is an important thought for those of us who have suffered in silence. In my case the person never was punished for this crime. It would ring in my ears for years that I needed justice.

But I had to allow God to handle that. God brings restoration, healing and forgiveness. In Isaiah 53 it speaks of Christ's sufferings and that it is only through his wounds that we receive healing. I never thought I would be able to forgive someone that took such a large chunk of my life. I thought of the battles my husband and I fought in marital intimacy. That residue tried to seep into every aspect of my life and make what God called pure, dirty. The freedom that I gained to be able to live with no visible, earthly justice came from constantly drawing from the father's well and learning his heart towards me.

Christ's sufferings and died for our freedom. He took on every single pain and hurt for us. There is so much love and compassion in Jesus Christ's sacrifice that I no longer feel as if I need to rush out to seek justice. God loves justice and hates injustice, per Isaiah 61:8. God was doing his beautiful work in and through my life. I walked in forgiveness and love and allowed God to be God in my situation.

MY FAITH WALK TODAY

Years into my adult life I met my husband, and I found myself feeling safe to share my past with him. It is amazing what God has waiting for us on the other side of hurt. I was met with so much love and acceptance that I could not even put it into words. For once I felt "fought for & defended". Just a friend at the time, this guy poured into me what God says about me. Although I heard it before, I was ready to receive the freedom that God wanted me to walk in. The call to freedom in our lives is no doubt the difference between the living and the dead. Think about how many of us spend our lives bound in the chains of shame, religion, hatred or any other form of oppression. It has been said that we serve a God who won't waste our pain and I believe that statement.

The more freedom I gained the more I understood what the enemy was afraid of. He was afraid that one day my feet would hit the ground and I would realize that I was not owned by my past. And the same God that delivered and healed me can deliver and heal you too!

WORDS OF ENCOURAGEMENT

Freedom is all an internal process and how we perceive our situation can shape the road that leads to our success. A huge step in your healing processes is forgiveness. You are defined only by God's love for you and not what someone did to you. Read Isaiah 61:10.

ABOUT THE AUTHOR

Kirstie Horton is married to Chauncy & one son, Knox. She holds a Bachelors in Business management. She has a passion to see people walk in the true freedom of Christ. She is a stay at home mom and owns an event design company. Contact Kirstie @ www.lefleurevents.com.

CHAPTER 27

BY HIS GRACE

Kimberly Armstrong

MY FAITH WAS TESTED

Christians often make references to Hell, but the sad reality is I lived through my own tormenting Hell, physically, mentally, emotionally, and spiritually. **My faith was tested** at a very early age. The childhood sexual abuse started early and lasted for several consecutive years. I experienced sexual abuse at the hands of an adult male, my neighbor, a family friend that grew up with my both of my parents, who also happened to be my babysitter's son. Ironically, he was the guy that all the neighbors loved and trusted.

He had a wife and a daughter. He taught me things he and his wife should have engaged in privately his goal was to teach me how to pleasure a man better than most grown women. He led me to believe it was all my fault and that I wanted it. I blamed myself for his predatory behavior. As my siblings began to age, I saw myself as their protector. When I noticed, his attention turned toward them I would sacrifice myself to keep him away from them. I had been violated, and boundaries had been obliterated. My life felt like hell on earth.

GOD REVIVED ME & REVEALED MY FAITH

I appreciate the sacrifice my mama made to care of all of us. Shortly thereafter, she helped my great aunt care for my uncle that was dying from cancer. And wanted me to live with them. My mom was hesitant, she eventually allowed me to live with my great auntie. This is how **God revived faith in me**! My auntie and I healed each other as our bond grew into a mother-daughter relationship. She got through her grief while God healed my pain of sexual abuse. My relationship with God was strengthened. I felt free, relieved, at peace, and innocent again.

MY FAITH WALK TODAY

My faith walk today is a constant journey. On Sunday evening June 19, 2016, I confronted the abuser from my childhood. I was determined to see that what happened in my past would no longer have rule over me. Nevertheless, I did what was best for ME. The chains were broken!

Having His apology, wasn't important to me. I was merely exhausted of avoiding him each time I went to visit my hometown. I had already forgiven him because I realize operating in unforgiveness does him no harm, but forgiveness releases me. His response was, "I forgive you, for what you made me do to you" What a blow, but God gave me peace during the storm!!

I am always honest with God about my shortcomings. I look to him for guidance in my life. I have found healing through therapy, and motivating myself to be a victor and not a victim. I will do anything within the will of God to stay mentally and emotionally healthy. I have my voice back, and I am determined to keep it!

I learned that I am worthy of God's love, I can set boundaries, release negative thoughts, grieve, tear down walls I had built, let go of destructive behaviors and care for myself without feeling guilty. Now I advocate for others who have yet to find their voice. My life has hope and full of adventures in self-discovery and loving myself imperfections and all.

WORDS OF ENCOURAGEMENT

My message to all survivors is Don't be afraid to face it. The good news is you can heal during your pain. Everyone cannot handle your truth, seek a licensed professional therapist never left you, and he will never abandon you. Lastly, and most importantly FORGIVE YOURSELF.

ABOUT THE AUTHOR

Kimberly Armstrong is an inspirational speaker. She advocates for the voiceless. KimArmstr@gmail.com for all speaking engagements.

XIV.
MARRIAGE & FAMILY

CHAPTER 28

LEARNING TO LET GO!

Teresa Hawley-Howard

MY FAITH WAS TESTED

In life, we all have hurts and pains and setbacks. I remember as a child my fondest memories were being at my grandparents' home. I loved it there. They spoiled me, told me I was smart. It was a refuge for me.

When I grandmother got sick, it brought up a lot of the past hurts and reasons why I was at their house non-stop. The pain of her passing was almost too much. I had lost someone who had guided me and loved me. And I was in a violent marriage. So, it seemed like a lifeline had been cut. And I was a drift in a sea of pain and agony. Daily just surviving not really living.

I was angry with God. How could he take her? I needed her. How could he leave me behind? It was almost unbearable. But at least I had my Grandpa left. He was my rock! But just 6 years later God called him home too. Now I had no lifeline, no cheering section, no more unfailing love and support! It was the hardest time. I knew they were together with God. My head knew this. But my heart was broken and angry.

<u>GOD REVIVED ME & REVEALED MY FAITH</u>

For almost 5 years I drifted from God. I worked three jobs and was raising my girls. And trying to survive in a domestic abusive marriage. I was running from God. And I was exhausted and hurting. The pain was constant in my heart and my body.

I was not even sure I wanted to go on. But I knew I could not leave my girls to fend for themselves. And I could not leave them with their Dad to raise them. So, I pushed on. I tried to find joy. I tried to smile. I tried to make a way and be happy. All to no avail.

But what some would call a tragedy, a shame, I called a gift from God. My teen daughter had a baby. That child gave me strength, a reason to get up and change. A reason to smile, a reason to live and a reason to step up in my role as Woman of God.

Little did I know that her and brother would give the strength and power just 5 years later to walk away from domestic violence. And the will and reason to change my life and to show them what love really was. I could hear my grandparents say You can do it. And I knew they were smiling down as I found my way back to God and back to me.

<u>MY FAITH WALK TODAY</u>

My life today is so different. I am loved by a wonderful man. And surrounded by my beautiful grandbabies. And I know God had plans for me, I just had to learn to let it go.

Holding on to pain and the past will block your blessings, keep you stagnant and not allow you to grow! You must forgive even when they are not sorry. It frees you not them.

I know my mission and my purpose! I know I am a powerful woman of God! He is in control and He is my source. Nothing else matters. He is in control. I finally learned to let go of the past and to embrace my future! I know God can change things in the blink of an eye! He can turn your mess into a message!

I am now a role model for my grandbabies and for all women and girls. I have been blessed to walk through my trials and tribulations and could use them to change the world. Each of us has a past and things we are not proud of and things that still haunt us. But when we let God's light shine in any corner of our life, He will erase our pains and hurts. I know He did it for me.

I am blessed today to be able to do what I love and make a living doing it. Helping women share their stories and testimonies. I know our words have power and can change the world one story at a time! So, don't hide your experiences. Use them to empower another. To uplift, inspire and encourage another.

I now wake up daily knowing God has as mission for me. He has a job for me. He has great plans for me. And until He calls me home, I will spend every day completing my mission.

Working on letting go of my past. Learning to forgive and move on. Helping others to learn the same. Reaching out to the hurting, the defeated, the forgotten and the survivors. Using what I have been delivered from to empower the next generation. Maybe they can learn from us and not have to burned by the same fire and sin. I certainly hope so.

I want to make sure I am an example of Christ's love!

When we learn to surrender our lives to God, He will use us to fulfill our calling, our place in the Kingdom, our role in this world. Each of us has our own special purpose. And we are the only ones who can complete it. So, step up and step out in faith. Someone is waiting on you.

I am thankful for all that I went through. I am thankful for all I survived. I am thankful for my trials and my detours and my wrong turns. These make of the woman I am today. And I LOVE HER! That statement was hard for me. For years, I could not say that. I was ashamed of the woman in the mirror. I did not like much less love her. But God changed that. If He could love and cherish me. All of me. All my flaws, my mistakes, and my scars. How could I not love her?

So, look and the mirror and tell yourself I love you!

WORDS OF ENCOURAGEMENT

Take time to get to know you. You are a child of God. He has great plans for you. The only one who can stop, delay or block your blessings is you. So, let go of the past and pain and move into your destiny.

You will go far in life when you walk in faith and in God's will. So, pray for guidance to hear God's plan for you. And then remember to listen. Plan your next move and then act. But first consult God!

ABOUT THE AUTHOR

Teresa Hawley-Howard is a wife, mom and Mimi. She lives in Texas with her wonderful husband, Rickey. He is the love of her life and a gift from God!

Her mission in life is to help other women discover the passion and purpose for her life. I also want to help her walk through her pain, her limitations, and her own doubt and live the life she deserves. I know our words, our stories, our scars, and our pain can inspire, heal and give hope to another woman.

You can reach her for speaking engagements, conferences, coaching and mentoring! www.teresahawleyhoward.com

teresa@takeactionwithteresa.com

CHAPTER 29

"REMOVING THE MASK ON MY ABUSE"

Pastor Clara L. Peters, TX, USA

This is not easy, however. after years of being in an unhealthy marriage, I realized this is not where I was called to be.

MY FAITH WAS TESTED

H owever, before the second child was born, I realized I was not in love with the one I was with. I settled as he was the father of my child, yet I was pregnant again, so what do I do? I must stay. I knew before I got pregnant with the second child that I really didn't want to be in this relationship any more however I wanted at least one more child because I wanted my children to have the same father. I always wanted to be married to the love of my life and have beautiful children, but after many years I realized I truly need to figure out a way to release myself from under the control I was in as he is truly not the love of my life.

By settling and not fulfilling my life's dream, I ended up in a very unhealthy, controlled relationship. We were together for twenty years.

After ten years, I was like okay Clara you must make a move. It took me a long time to even speak out loud that I was abused mentally and physically along with being controlled. I was afraid to say it out loud as if it was my fault then I realized I didn't do anything wrong but allowed that to go on. I prayed, and I knew this is not the life GOD had ordained for me, so I asked him to help me to come out of it.

GOD REVIVED ME & REVEALED MY FAITH

As my faith in God began to grow even stronger, I finally realized I can do it if I seek Him, and he will give me the courage to face all trails or tribulations that may come my way. So, in 2001, I said no more to being abused, no more to being controlled, and no more to being used for what he wanted. I do have dreams, and I do have wants. I do have needs of my own, and I am ready to obtain them.

Who should live like that, nobody? I had to find my voice. I had to say no more to being in bondage and no more to living a life of being afraid in my own home.

It took me four years to complete the leave, but I did it with a lot of pain. Yet, it was the pain worth having, for I was not being controlled or abused anymore.

As it is stated in Romans 12:2, "Do not be conformed to this world, but be transformed by the renewal of your mind, that by testing you may discern what is the will of God, what is good and acceptable and perfect."

This means that as your transformation is being done, a metamorphosis will occur. Let's look at the caterpillar and how it becomes a butterfly. The caterpillar is in its shell, and as it is working its way out of that shell, it becomes a cocoon and then a butterfly.

The stages of the butterfly start with it being an egg, a caterpillar, a cocoon, and then the butterfly. As a human, your stages may be of being in that shell of control, deciding on becoming you, moving into you, and then being you.

Let me give you a real-life scenario. As you enter a relationship and you commit yourself wholeheartedly to that relationship, what if that commitment turns into someone controlling you? After you come to your senses, you realize this is not how it supposes to be, so you take it upon yourself to take back your life. What you did is work your way out of that shell and set yourself free to be you.

You can obtain this transformation by choosing to be transformed from your old ways and becoming that new you, by seeking God's words and living it, and by believing God will transform you.

Pray as it is stated in Matthew 7:7, "Ask and it will be given to you; seek and you will find; knock and the door will be opened to you." And lastly, you can obtain transformation by your vision, so write it down and follow it.

To be happy with your life, you need to have your own identity and love yourself. We sometimes wear a mask hiding that beautiful life as a loving marriage is not the truth. It was time for me to take off the mask(s). My family was shocked, for they had no idea.

Remove that mask, and start being the person you were born to be. God did not put us here to be in bondage and do what others choose for us to be or do. Set yourself free, and know God is waiting for you to remove the mask and become that woman He designed for you to be. Removing the mask may take some fasting, praying, and just seeking

God. The only way you are going to be able to do it successfully is to step out on faith and know God has you.

Find out your heart's desire and start working on what that is. If you need training, go back to school. Do whatever it will take, so you can become who and what God designed for you and your life.

However, as a wife and mother we will always be the PROVERBS 31 woman. Get to know you, and I promise you, you will love you and realize things you did not know about yourself. It is a good feeling to be able to be you per God and not what others want you to be.

WORDS OF ENCOURAGEMENT

My prayer is that each woman that reads this or hear my journey of abuse make a commitment with self NOW to start loving and learning you. Look in the mirror and tell yourself daily, "Girl, I just love me some you." Your life will be so much better, and it will be better for those around you too.

2 Corinthians 3:17 states "Now the Lord is the Spirit, and where the Spirit of the Lord is, there is freedom," so go after your freedom.

God has shared with me that he wants each one I connect with to know that you must sometimes go through the wilderness to see the greatness he has for you. I was like but why then he said look at the big picture my daughter.

I encourage you to not let your yesteryears stop you from being restored into what God, not man but God, has promised you what he has just for you.

Being you per God is a wonderful feeling. The weight was lifted from my shoulders, and I could truly live. It took me forty years, but I thank God I can live. I have my voice, and I have my wings now. The world is mind as I do the work of my Father. I tell you I love being the authentic me he designed me to be.

MY FAITH WALK TODAY

What am I doing now? I'm living life to the fullest loving like I never loved before. And I am laughing as if it is my last breath and enjoying being the woman my Father wants me to be.

He said Clara you are the VOICE for the VOICELESS and you must help as many as you can find their voice find their way to becoming their true AUTHENTIC Self.

ABOUT THE AUTHOR

I am the Founder of Women of Divine Distinction Ministry, Women of Divine Distinction Blog Talk Radio Show, The Authentically YOU Life Coach and Divine Diva Book Club.

You can connect with me via Facebook at Clara L Peters, my website is www.womenofdivinedistinction.com, my email is wodd.2011@yahoo.com

I am blessed to be called mother by 2 daughters and 1 son all grown and the G.momma to 6 (2 girls and 4 boys) grandchildren who are the reason I breathe. I am a pastor, mentor, motivational speaker, blog talk radio show host, blogger, international bestselling author, life coach, peer recovery coach, Christian counselor and God's daughter. I am a woman of integrity that is blessed to be the VOICE for the VOICELESS.

CHAPTER 30

FAITH IN FAMILY

Demetria Kossie TX, USA

MY FAITH WAS TESTED

When I'm alone I break down and cry, I always felt that my mother didn't love me, I would give my life for my mother, being the baby of five children, I dedicated my life, my time, my energy, my everything, to begin there for my mother, and I'm the one she treated so bad and always made fun of, I have never questioned God about anything I just kept doing what was right for her.

But this one time, on Thanksgiving Day me, and my husband Charles and our four children, arrived at my Mother's house, everyone else had already made it there, we walked into the house and the entire room just stared at us, we spoke to everyone, and out of nowhere my Mother burst out and say, "Here comes the poor family" and everyone just burst out laughing! I was so hurt, and shame I told my husband get the kids and come on, I turned and walked out the door, tears started streaming down my face, because we were always treated differently, and always the target to be picked on because we didn't drive a nice car, and live in a fine home like the others, we walked home hurt, shame, and crying my eyes out, I could not stomach this, it was to hurtful, and I could see the hurt in my husband and kids eyes We made it home, I went into the bathroom and cried I asked myself why? Why me? I thought about taking my own life.

GOD REVIVED ME & REVEALED MY FAITH

While In the bathroom figuring out how I was going to end my life, a voice just came into the bathroom and said "I Love You" I stood up, looked behind the shower curtain thinking someone was playing games, then I looked into the mirror and the image of Jesus was standing behind me, I couldn't move, then that is when I heard him **say**, "I Love You" and he faded away, I dried my eyes to see if the image was still there, but it was gone but the voice still echoed throughout the bathroom, I washed my face and stood up tall and I said "Lord if you Love me so why do you let my family hurt me so bad?"

I sat down on the side of the bathtub and dropped my head, and then that same voice spoke to me again saying " you said you believe in me and my words" my body just went numb, tears started to fall down my face again, and my mind went straight to the Bible, and I started saying verses out the Bible, all of a sudden I begin to praise God, and I got a tingling sensation and God told me that my Father, Mother, Sister and my Brother, I could not stop Praising God, and God assured me that he will never leave me, nor forsaken me.

MY FAITH WALK TODAY

A year has passed since my family was humiliated in front of everyone, I had not seen or spoken to any of my family members, and yes it does hurt, but God gave me the strength to lean and trust in him, and he will be my family. I got back into church, and rededicated my life, and that was the best thing I could have done for me and my family, my Faith today is so strong until when family and friends hurt you just trust in God and he will bring you through any hurtful situation and he will be the family you need, and I do not put my trust and confidence in family.

I put my Faith in God and I know he will be right by my side, but I would like to start Speaking on Keeping the Faith, I almost gave up on my entire life due to the fact my Faith was weak and I did not know how to fight this Spiritual thing, and it was trying to take me out, but God came and rescued me.

I already had the weapons to fight this monster but I was weak, but to-day my Faith Walk is so strong, I do not let anyone or anything get me down or make me sad, and that stands for family and friends, if they do not want me in their lives, just fine with me, that is their loss, I'm going to keep trusting in God and keeping the Faith over my life, I know it will not be easy all the time but I will keep believing, and trusting, and I do know when people make fun of you, and hurt your feelings just smile at them, cause you know you have a mighty friend called Jesus. And he will never let you down.

WORDS OF ENCOURAGEMENT

No matter how bad a situation may seem, if you keep the Faith, and Trust God everything will work out for your good, Satan is out to steal, kill, and destroy it is up to you to stop him in his tracks, storms will occur. but with Faith the Size of a mustard seed you can ride the storm out, and when it stops raining the sun will shine again. when Love ones hurt, you forgive them, God forgave you, and you must forgive to get to Heaven, and to receive your Blessings. Be respectful to your parents, cause the Bible tells me that you should Honor your mother and father or your days will be shortened, yes, our parents make us sad and mad at times, but they should not be disrespected in no kind of way, when you know you have hurt someone please go to that person and tell them "I was wrong I am sorry"

ABOUT THE AUTHOR

Demeteria Kossie   43yrs old, writing has been my passion since I was a kid, I'm marries to a wonderful man named Charles been married for 21years, we have 4 amazing children, and 4 amazing grandchildren, I'm an Author and co-author I'm also an Event Planner my book can be purchased online on Amazon "The Beaten Face" my email address is kossied@yahoo.com

CHAPTER 31

FINDING A FOREVER
HOME...

Ingrid Edwards, TX, USA

MY FAITH WAS TESTED

When I wanted to adopt the baby of our foster daughter. I nurtured, loved, and bonded with this unborn baby for 6 months until birth during the pregnancy of my 12-year-old foster daughter. I thought that this was to be the newest addition to our family another son sent from God... My husband and I had already adopted three kids one girl and two boys.... But years later CPS placed a pregnant 12 yrs. old with us. She gave birth at age 13 and decided she wanted to keep her baby. During her pregnancy, I home schooled her and made sure she and this unborn would in the best of health. The closest a woman comes to death is in child birth and she was no woman she was 13 when we delivered. This baby Had become my everything the only thing I didn't do was conceive or deliverer him. On paper, I was responsible.

Once home from the hospital he slept in my room I wake up every three hours to feed him because at 13 my foster daughter was not responsible enough to care for her newborn and she was suffering with postpartum depression. I would wake her up to feed him and she would lay him down next to her and go back to sleep. During the next six weeks during her recovery, I tried to make her bond we him giving her more responsibility taking care of him. She was feeding him and changing him we had made great progress. Now it was time for her to go to school, she did well in school and was a smart. Boys would be our down fall. The baby is now crawling than walking and talking before we know it two years had passed. It was now time to look from a place that would take mother and baby.

We searched the entire Houston and surrounding areas, no one would take both they wanted one or the other but not mother and baby. The CPS worker found a place that would take mother and baby but it was in San Antonio Texas. We were very excited about this placement our babies were going to be together and our 13-year-old would get to see what being a mother was truly about and the sacrifices that She would have to make.

My daughter would call me crying stating the baby was sick and she wasn't allowed to go to school she had to stay home and take of him. I explained to her on many occasions that mother's sacrifice everything to care for their babies especially when they're sick. The baby's needs come before everything else. She would say he was awake crying all night and nobody would come and get him so she could get some sleep. I would try to explain to her that he was her responsibility and the staff was only there to assist her with him, not to take care of him because she was sleepy.

The staff assured me that they were monitoring the situation closely and she was tired and did not want to care for her son who has another ear infection. She had missed about nine days of school because he had been sick and with fever, which means no daycare and mom is left to her for him with supervision. Eventually placement broke down baby return home to us 13-year-old placed in a girl's facility. Now without a doubt I wanted to adopt this baby in my heart he was already family and I loved him like a gave him life I nurtured him in the womb until birth then every day all day when she attended School. So clearly my husband saw this love and bond the baby and one shared. However, when the question came up about adoption his answer was always the same NO not going to happen... My husband had stated on many occasions we are not adopting him.

My husband told me not to take him back when CPS called to inform us that they needed to leave San Antonio. But my husband eventually gave in and allowed me to bring him home. The baby would be moving over to the adoption side of CPS within the year and we would need to decide within the next six months. I prayed, the baby prayed, the family prayed I think even the CPS worker, and my agency worker was praying. I cried and fell into a deep depression my husband answer was still the same NO... When the time came for my baby to be adopted I was crazy with anger and hurt I lost all hope and faith...I didn't understand how God could allow these to happen. It was like my heart had been ripped out of my chest and I was devastated. I thought that this could cost us our marriage.

GOD REVIVED ME & REVEALED MY FAITH!

Prayer Changes Things

I prayed, the baby prayed, the family prayed, I cried, I fast and then I became depression my husband answer was still the same NO... During the past year while the baby was gone we had fostered many children some were new and some at been with us the entire duration. We are a foster to adopt home and all the kids that we get are up for adoption. We foster girls and boys ages ranged from newborn to 17. We had foster boys and girls that wanted us to adopt them and they understood that we were not adopting and that they would be with us until CPS found them a forever home. So, now the baby is back and he is walking and talking up a storm. The family is torn everyone loves him and don't want to see him go.

My husband saw the change in me and said that we needed to talk about how my love for the baby was consuming me and everyone could see it. I asked him if he loved to baby he said yes.... I loves all our kids Not just him and I am going to hate to see him leave just as a hate to see them all go. But this is not about me or you this is about finding them all a family and a FOR EVER HOME.... I knew then without a doubt that this adoption was not going to happen.

Nevertheless, I didn't understand why he allowed me to bring my baby back home. Hurt and feeling like I had been lead on I asked my husband why did he let me bring him back home? My husband slowly look up at me, standing to close for comfort, he took two steps backwards and then said.... I know you needed to make sure he was okay and I also wanted to let him know we love him and We will be his Papa and Nana forever.

I also wanted you to have some closure if possible and to be a part of the process of finding his new parents and his forever home......Now!!!!! You know DAMN well I was NOT EXPECTING HIM TO SAY THIS incredibly, wonderful and passionate words of wisdom to me.... ONLY GOD.... I was expecting ignorance and selfishness !!!!!...I WAS READY TO FIGHT... but my arms were too short to fight with God!!!!! even though we have our problems, God knows we do, I LOVE THIS MAN and he LOVES ME BACK....See I was so busy worrying about my own pain that I didn't realize that my husband was hurting too and I called him the selfish one, my GOD.

The time is coming for our baby to be adopted I was crazy with anger, I had lost faith and my husband Had become the enemy. Faith.

I always believe that things will turn out the way I think they should. Oh, my GOD I had it all wrong... I went inside my closet and got on my knees that didn't work so stretched-out on the floor. I had been so selfish, angry, bitter, unhappy, uncaring, untouchable and unlovable. I fell asleep in the closet; my husband dares not touch me to awake me placed a blanket over me and left me there. During the mist of my sleep God reveal to me what my grandmother used to say to me all the time... what God has for you... is for you... and if this baby was meant to ours nothing would have been able to stop it from happening.

I could see the faces of all the foster children that we have fostered that would have given anything for us to be there forever parents and un-equivocally the answer was no we were not adopting. I am now awakening and I could not imagine explaining to my kids why we were adopting the baby but we could not adopt them. My Lord what an awesome God we serve, He truly does make a way out of no way. He spoke to me while I was sleeping so that I could not interrupt and I could clearly see his vision and understand.

MY FAITH WALK TODAY

One Day at A Time...

Our baby was adopted by a wonderful family and during his transition into his forever family and forever home. We could talk to him and I could sing to him before he went to bed. I thank God for that opportunity and for choosing us for such a life changing experience. The closest a woman comes to death is in childbirth and she was not a woman she was a child only 12 years old when this journey began and 13 when the baby was born. There is not a day go by that I don't think of them or miss them both. Our foster daughter has run away multiple times from many different facilities and homes.

She has been in a facility for girls in San Antonio and was doing so well that her leveled had dropped and she would need to be moved soon. Her caseworker was looking for her home in the Houston area for her but didn't want to bring she back in town and was very skeptical even though she promised she wouldn't run away again. I explained to CPS they should try to keep her in that area if possible because She was doing so well there. My daughter was bipolar and a runaway if she got back to town we're friends and relatives live she was going to run again and she did. She is currently being missing in action. On the other hand, (her son) our baby is doing remarkably well even taking piano lessons.

This experience changed my life it and made me aware that God still testing me. God, he has greater plans for my future I must be able to deal with Heartbreak, Devastation, Loss and maybe even Death. I am growing in my faith and my walk-in faith, I have daily struggles with the truth as it is vs what I want it to be. I know that "I pair of lips will say anything" and reality is much different than the words or promises that people will make to get want they want. I know this because I am a living witness to this today. I must prepare myself for the many Storms that coming to fully can appreciate the reward that GOD has for my life. My prayer daily is Father God let your will be done not mine ...I am selfish and I want what I want when I want it help me to accept you will and give me the strength to carry on.

WORDS OF ENCOURAGEMENT

My FAITH, life struggles, my mouth, my love, my lack of trust, my disappointments, my pride and my passion has placed me in different levels of depression in my young Life. I know God is not through with me yet which means the devil will not leave me alone... God continues to bless my life and he has given me many testimonies, alone with undeniable faith that is driving me forward and preparing me for battles and struggles ahead. I encourage every reader to pray and get to know the power of prayer. Prayer is only a conversation between you and God... God will deliverer you out of whatever you may be going through, pray to God and watch him make changes in your life know that there is great power in his word. Prayer Changes Things...

ABOUT THE AUTHOR

Ingrid Edwards is a native of Texas and resides with her husband and children. She is foster parent, a grandmother, business owner, realtor, and an international bestselling author.

XV.
LIVING WITH
LOSS IN FAITH

CHAPTER 32

CRASHING INTO FAITH

Annisha Lawrence Dones, GA, USA

MY FAITH WAS TESTED!

My life would seem to be at a halt after I received a call. A call that I thought would be fatal to my faith. The night seemed to be regular until I received information about my fiancé. I was awestruck by the information I received. My entire life would come crumbling down with that one phone call. I would receive the news that my soon to be husband had just been killed on impact in a car accident. Not only would I be faced with loss and grief but I would have to deal with the loss and grief that my son would experience due to the absence of a father. Many emotions ran through my mind on that night. I began to question all that I had been taught and I often asked myself, "why me?" If ever you find yourself asking "why me?", you know that you are in for a long haul to revive something that is dead. This was an overwhelming feeling for me, my life indeed had been shattered into pieces. My fiancé brought in the bulk of our income and he was the backbone of our family. When his life ended, it seems as if my faith ended as well. I believed that the Lord couldn't have loved me because I had lost something so dear to me. I often struggled with depression and hopelessness after the crash but I knew that I had to continue to move forward for my children. It seemed to me that the enemy had gotten me offended at God. I had an unexplained anger in my heart for the things of God and I felt that the Lord had forsaken my family and me. Although I say the anger was unexplained, I can now see that it was unforgiveness towards God. It was clear that I had lost more than the love of my life, I had lost my faith!

GOD REVIVED ME & REVEALED MY FAITH!

There were days that I was consumed by tears of frustration. I felt like I had been ripped completely of everything that was good in my life. At the time, I did not know that I had lost so much hope. It is funny how the same thing that came to break you, can help to make you stronger. I spent years questioning God and questioning the death of my fiancé'. The Lord had to restore my faith in him but it would not happen in an unconventional way. There were years that I believed that I would never believe again. Another Crash happened! This time, my faith would collide into my future life as a Christian.

God revealed faith to me through another crash. This time it would be my son! My son was involved in a very serious car accident years after my husband died. Every time I receive news that someone has been an accident my heart stops from the fear that I will never see that person again. It was like that for me when I received the news that my son was in accident. Time stopped! Although my son was in a very serious car accident that left him in critical condition for some time, God revived him and restored him. My mother and my family were praying for my son to live and not die! God answered those prayers although the doctors believed that his life was going to end. The prayers availed much.

As I knelt to pray the day that I received that news, somehow, somewhere deep down inside of me, I knew that he would live. This was God revealing to me that his hand was still on my life, even though I was angry with him for all those years. He was showing me that the same thing the enemy used to destroy your faith, I will use to restore your faith! You are indeed taken care of. Not only did God restore my faith but he restored my son to full health. Today, my son looks as if he has never been in a car accident before.

His face is without blemish and my heart is without trouble. My faith was tested but through that test God revealed things to me that I would not be able to comprehend or understand then, that I can now understand. Sometimes it takes a traumatic event to learn that God's hand has never left your life. God restored my faith!

MY FAITH WALK TODAY!

God restored my faith! Today God has made a way for me to experience joy. I still love my fiancé and miss him. But he has restored my family and he has restored my faith. I love the Lord and know that he is faithful to me. I can trust him and I believe that he will cause all things to work out for my good. The Lord has been faithful in providing for me and helping to meet all my needs. My faith may have gone through a long testing but God brought me through all the pain and tragedy that the enemy tried to put in my way.

WORDS OF ENCOURAGEMENT!

God will turn your tragedy around. Always remember that God is faithful and he will not let you down, no matter what you may face.

ABOUT THE AUTHOR

Annisha is from Atlanta, Ga. She has faithfully worked in the hotel industry for years. She is a mother of 3 beautiful children. She is a songwriter and a singer and enjoys LIFE!

CHAPTER 33

UNWAVERING FAITH

Tristan Jackson, TX, USA

MY FAITH WAS TESTED:

I was raised in a small low income neighborhood near downtown Houston by a single parent. My lifelong lesson has been to find my own identity in this sometimes crazy and very harsh world. I work extra hard in high school. I had to work even harder in college. But through God grace and hard work, I graduated college. The only child out of eight siblings to attend college and graduate.

During the month of July 2016. My faith has been tested in my areas of my life. Imagine losing your job in one week. The next week, you see your cousin killed. Oh yes, July 2016 was the month my Faith was tested even the more. Faith is the substance of things hoped for and the evidence of things not seen. Faith may be something different to everyone. I felt that, like a swimmer swimming upstream, against the currents. With losing my cousin, and my job within a week times.

We were taught as a child to go to school, go to college, and get your degree, gain experience, get a good job with benefits, and you will be set for life. Yes, that is true until you get that unexpected phone call from upper management. Sorry, miss Jackson 7-28-16, we will be terminating your contact. I questioned God, "what in the world is going on in my life? Why did that happen to me?

Imagine talking to someone and laughing with them, and less than 5 minutes later, you see running and hear screaming. Kids screaming, adults running, fireworks going off! You hear bullets and screams. You watch your cousin take his last breath. Shot dead in front of the family and myself. I questioned the lord, why. Why did they have to leave us so early? We needed more time to spend with them.

Death is not easy to deal with. Even those losing my job and cousin, I still had one thing which was my faith. I knew that God was taking me through the storm. Faith is an expression of hope for something better.

GOD REVIVED ME & REVEALED MY FAITH :

I grew in the church, and I would listen to elder talk about God, faith, and the storms of life. It was until my recent storm, that God revived my faith. During my storm, I am beyond grateful that God provides hope and I held onto my faith. And through this faith test I've learned 2 strategies to mitigate my fear and sense of hopelessness and helped grow with my faith. I had to get my prayer life back in order. God revealed that, this storm was built to strength my life.

Strategy 1: is prayer. Prayer is the portal that connects us to the true and living God. Sometimes we need heaven to rain down on our earthly situation. The Bible teaches us that we are to pray without ceasing. The second strategy is praise your way through the storm. Out of all the strategies, praising God has help me. Sometimes during trials and tests we must say, "Hallelujah anyhow." Job said it best, "Yet though they slay me, I will still praise HIM."

MY FAITH WALK TODAY

Through this short story about Faith, I shared with you my own faith experience the journey with Christ which started as a young child and has continued to this day. I admitted that my faith journey has been both rewarding and difficult. My faith walk today is much different prior to July 2016.

My story is called unwavering faith. What is unwavering faith? When something is unwavering, it is firm or unshakable. If you're a good hockey goalie, then you'll show an unwavering determination to keep the puck out of your goal. Just as it sounds, the word unwavering refers to something that will not waver, wander, or go astray.

Although I have many reasons for believing, the ultimate one is the inner testimony of my heart. Somehow, I just know what I know. I have an inner confidence that has stayed strong for many years despite all the ways it's been tested. This is the testimony of the Holy Spirit opening my spiritual eyes to the truth. He sent the storm of losing a cousin and job, within a week time to test my faith.

WORDS OF ENCOURAGEMENT

Matthew 21:21

21 Jesus replied, "Truly I tell you, if you have faith and do not doubt, not only can you do what was done to the fig tree, but also you can say to this mountain, 'Go, throw yourself into the sea,' and it will be done.

Inspiration and Strength

Isaiah 41:10 fear not, I am with you; be not dismayed, for I am your God; I will strengthen you, I will help you, I will uphold you with my righteous right hand.

Jeremiah 29:11:

For I know the plans I have for you, declares the LORD, plans for welfare and not for evil, to give you a future and a hope.

ABOUT AUTHOR

Tristan Jackson earned her Bachelors of Business Administration in Human Resource Management (2009) and Masters of Public Administration (2013) from Lamar University. She loves God and helping her family. She is the owner of T.J.'s & more located in Houston, Texas.

Accomplishments:

•Bachelors of Business Administration Human Resource Management Masters of Public Administration.

•Business Owner: 2014-Present, T.J. & More

Email: Jackson_tristan@yahoo.com

Website: http://tjsandmore.com

XVI

EVERY SINGLE PERSON SHOULD HEAR THIS !

CHAPTER 34

GOD DELIVERED ME

Shonte' Te'Ola Johnson, Ruston, La

MY FAITH WAS TESTED

There have been numerous events during my life that have challenged me as a person and tested my faith as a Woman of God. The most memorable time takes me back to a tumultuous relationship that often made me ponder, was I deserving of God's constant love for me when I was clearly allowing myself to be in a position that was not pleasing to Him. I lived with a man that was not my husband, took care of a home without the benefit of marriage which led to a dark space in my mind and heart. I often found myself not wanting to pray because I felt I had let God down so much with what I wanted to do and He probably would not hear the prayers of a constant sinner.

Several things happened within the relationship that I felt as if I deserved because of what I was doing. I felt favor and grace were very far from my life and things were spiraling out of control. I was not happy at home, I could not find happiness on the job, my finances were suffering and I felt as if I could not talk to family because of fear of judgement or they simply would not try to understand. The feelings and thoughts of loneliness seemed to be my new way of life.

It was not until I hit rock bottom that I realized the God, I felt so distant from was the same God that held me close even when I felt I was not deserving of his love. I made the decision to lean on Him, it was at that point that everything I did not have a clue about were spiritually revealed to me. I asked God to remove people that were not around for my good to be removed. It was that moment that walls came down, doors were opened and life as I knew it was renewed.

GOD REVIVED ME & REVEALED MY FAITH

God's grace and mercy revived and revealed my faith through constant talks with Him, answered prayers and a release of all the stressors that held me bound. Again, my prayer to remove people that did not have my best interest at heart as well as anything that hindered my relationship with God. The first person, He removed was the person I thought I connected with the most (my ex-boyfriend). AS I look back over my life, I cannot understand why I did not see he was not the person for me.

While leaning on God, I now understand I was allowing my heart to lead me down a path, my mind and spirit knew were not right for me. It was seeing things through my spiritual eyes that have shown me, I deserve the best out of life and that means I must now embrace the gift/blessing of being a single Woman of God. The first man, I need to focus on, is the first one who loves me unconditionally. When we feel the warmth of God's love, we do not accept anything less from any other man.

The only relationship I want to build on most is the same one that has sustained me throughout this journey called life. Through my faith, I feel I have a new lease on life and I will not allow the stress of anyone nor anything to bring me to a point of darkness ever again. When I feel as if I cannot see my way, faith is the one thing that gives me strength to hold on a little while longer. I would use the word faith to encourage anyone to depend on during the times in life when we feel a storm raging. Faith can be our shield to protect us and help us to see the bright side of our darkest days.

MY FAITH WALKED TODAY

My life today has been changed in more ways than I could have ever imagined. My smile today is genuine and honestly feels like my best asset. I smile because I know what I have been through but most important, I know the reason I am still here. The love of God is more than sufficient and has helped me to see the sunshine when I never thought it would have been possible to see. I know understand that I do not have to go anything alone because God will be a friend and answer when I call even in the midnight hours.

There is no point to worry about anything when I can pray about everything. As I think back to what God has done for me, I am reminded of the scripture from: Psalm 46:1 "God is our refuge and strength, an ever-present help in trouble". With God on my side, I am more than a conqueror and I do not have to worry about being alone when He is there to help me through anything I may face. I encourage anyone feeling down or seeking refuge from the stressors of life to try God and watch Him make a difference in your life. There are no prayers He will not answer and no storm He cannot calm.

When we are sinners and living in our sins, He can bring us out from among the things that are holding us back from having a divine relationship with Him. When we ask Him to remove things that hinder us, we must brace ourselves for the people that must leave. No relationship that is right for us will cause a strain on the relationship we have with God. His timing is perfect and He knows the desires of our heart when we allow Him in our lives.

<u>WORDS OF ENCOURAGEMENT</u>

The best advice I would give to any young woman that finds herself struggling with faith, relationships and sin is to first seek God. Maintain a daily conservation with Him, pray always and know that when you are at your lowest points, He will be there to pick you up again. Any relationship with a man that does not have God in his life is not the right man to be with.

A man who loves God will always ensure he is doing right by you not only will his words show you but his actions will prove it. As a Woman of God, we know that God has a divine plan for our lives and sin should never be allowed to distance our walk with Him. Love God and love yourself, hide yourselves in Him so that any man who finds you, will find Him because He dwells in the deepest crevices of our hearts.

ABOUT THE AUTHOR

Shonte' Te'Ola Johnson is from Jonesville, La. She resides in Ruston, La and is a retail banker. She's dedicated to God's work as an exhorter and loves all people. Her life goal is to have a closer walk with God.

CHAPTER 35

FREE INDEED

Nikki Jackson, TX, USA

MY FAITH WAS TESTED

I endured a marriage for 9 years! I was in love with a man that would ultimately try to destroy me with his fist. I was married and endured physical abuse. I tried to trust God but often felt like God was not hearing me for a period of 9 years. I knew that God was punishing me, or at least this is how I felt. I thought that I was cursed and I thought that because I lived a lifestyle that was not pleasing to God before I was married, God was getting back at me in a way. I knew that this guy came into my life to curse it when I endured the heartache. He would hit me and kick me in my face, I would survive many rounds of guns to my head, slaps and pushes to my face and punches to my heart.

As I continued in the marriage, my heart began to grow colder to the things of God. I got away from God, because I never understood how God could allow this to happen to me. I was angry with God, miserable and hurt. I would consume pills to try and numb the pain but it only got worse. This would lead to depression and low self-esteem. This was my reality. My husband would torment me, torture me, and abuse me. It went on so long that I lost faith! Many wondered why I stayed but the fear of being alone and surviving tormented me. Fear of being a single parent with 3 children and that I could not make it was a terrifying thing to me, I thought I could not make it on my own. I would wonder where the finances would come from. He would always threaten my life when I tried to walk away or would always say phrases like, "I will kill you if you leave." But after he tried to take my life the day after Christmas and I knew that I could not stay in that relationship. I knew that if I stayed, I would be the next victim of domestic violence.

GOD REVIVED ME & REVEALED MY FAITH

As time progressed I would hear stories from women in the same situation I was in, they would tell me the stories about how they would have pain in their marriages for 20 plus years. It was terrible. After one friend telling me about a marriage that she was still in after 20 years, I knew that I did not want that to be me! God begin to reveal things to me and I prayed. God wanted to remove me from the situation, but I kept going back after praying.

After about 8 years, I would question God, cry out to God and ask, "why me?" I was in my back yard when God spoke to me and said, "why not you?" I started studying spiritual books and begin to read books about marriage. I realized that it was not me, it was him! I begin to pray and seek after answers. I knew that my pain would birth my purpose ultimately and that I would find beauty through all of this somehow.

After dealing with him for a long time, I had enough! I started to trust God and left! I did not look back, I looked to my future and begin to press through the pain. I started to move towards my purpose. Philippians 3:14 states, "I press toward the mark for the prize of the high calling of God in Christ Jesus." God saved me and said that if I trusted him, he would do the impossible in my life. I knew that I would be okay.

I went through a healing process for 18 months and although it was not easy, a huge part of my healing process was telling my story! I would share my story about how God freed me and how I am free indeed. God made everything that I thought was wrong with me, right! I begin to love myself and I begin to love God again when I left. God really freed me on the inside and on the outside!

MY FAITH WALK TODAY

I have a great relationship with God today! God has restored me in more than one way! He has strengthened me in my inner woman and given me all that I need and more. I am so happy today. I am thriving in all my relationships. I am working in the church, serving God without reservations. I am stronger in the Lord. I love the Lord more and I understand God more on a level I did not understand before now in this new faith walk I am stronger, spiritually, and emotionally and no longer living under that emotional abuse of a broken man. I am no longer in fear for my life and I am walking in purpose! My faith walk today is amazing because I walk with God at the head of my life.

WORDS OF ENCOURAGEMENT

To every woman that have been in a situation like mine, please know your worth and trust God through the process. Know that it gets better. Have faith and know there is a full life after pain and divorce.

ABOUT THE AUTHOR

Nikki Jackson is a servant of God, successful business woman, she's an entrepreneur of a foster home, domestic violence non-profit that serves male and female victims and Her latest project is a transition home for women dealing with domestic violence. Nikki loves to travel and is the mother of 3 beautiful children.

XVII.
FAITH IN
POLITICS

CHAPTER 36

UNBREAKABLE FAITH

Judge Maria T. Jackson

TX, USA

MY FAITH WAS TESTED

My faith has been tested many times. But there are two times that are in the forefront of my mind. I will share them with you.

I had my first child at 35 years old. I had an emergency C-Section, and my son and I almost died. The Doctors didn't think either one of us were going to survive. The nurses told me that I would be released in 6 days because that is what my insurance would allow. However, they told me that my son would not be going home with me because he was too ill and he was still in ICU. I looked at the nurses and told them that my son would leave the hospital with me. I prayed to God fervently, and every day the Dr. would give me progress on my son. The second day he told me the fluid in my son's lungs were gone. There was progression every day, and on the seventh day my son came home with me. God is Good!

The second one that comes to mind is when I was serving as a Municipal Court Judge and The Democratic Party asked me to run for State District Judge. No one believed in me, even the people in my inner circle. The only ones that believed in me were myself, my parents, and God. I am now serving my third term as the 339th State District Judge where I preside over serious felony offenses and several of my Capital Murder trials have been featured on National Television shows. I have learned that when God places a desire in your heart, go for it! If God is for you, who can be against you??

<u>GOD REVIVED ME & REVEALED MY FAITH</u>

Lessons were learned for me in marriage as, I was unequally yoked in both of my previous marriages. When we marry, we must pray about it, seek God for guidance in our decisions I gave God a list of the qualities I wanted in a man. God knew my heart and my needs better than I did. So, I did not date for five years. I focused on my children, myself and my career.

I decided to take a break on dating to get to know me, spend more time with my 2 boys and concentrate on my job. That break turned into five years. After the fifth year, I started saying aloud, "Okay God it's been five years now and I am ready to date. A couple of nice guys came along and I would go to dinners and enjoy myself. I had given God my list of what type of man I wanted many years ago, and I almost started to believe that my expectations were too high. But God! Let me say it again, But God!

The Love of my life showed up. His name is Frank. We had crushes on each other in Junior High. We never dated, we were just casual friends. We grew up a block away from each. He asked if his son could intern for me because he is interested in becoming an Attorney. I didn't hesitate to say "Yes" because I love to mentor our young people.

Frank came to my court and he was such a pleasant surprise. He is tall, has broad shoulders and very handsome. He asked to take me out for dinner and I didn't hesitate to say yes to that either. Our second date Frank asked if we could date exclusively. I was a little shocked because I wasn't used to a man being so open and honest about his feelings. I needed to sleep on that big decision. The next day I called Frank and said Yes! I would like to be in an exclusive relationship with you". Well that was one of the best decisions I made for my future with God's guidance. Frank and I are now happily married.

God sent me exactly what I needed. An honest man, a man to love me completely. Someone to share the ups and downs with. Someone to walk through this world with. Someone to spend time with. Someone who loves me unconditionally. And someone to Follow God's plan with me.

I am truly blessed and thankful! God knew exactly who I needed. And in his perfect timing he sent him to me. So always know God's timing is perfect. So, pray and prepare and God will make a way if it is in God's will and time.

MY FAITH WALK TODAY

I have had my share of ups and downs. My share of triumphs and disappointments. My share of heartbreaks and fears. We all have them. I am no different. But I have learned to never lose faith. Never give up. Never stop trying. Always look up to God. He has you! And he won't let you down!

I know God will always let me finish the work had me begin. He has great plans for each of us.

He tells us in his word. For I know the plans I have for you," declares the LORD, "plans to prosper you and not to harm you, plans to give you hope and a future. Jeremiah 29:11

As a State District, Criminal Court Judge, my goal is to make a difference every day. We need to lead our youth by example. They are our future. It's a serious position, I preside over serious felony offenses. This position carries a load of responsibility. I know I am changing lives and making a difference in this world daily. This position is a major blessing. God placed me in this position and I serve as his steward.

I am also blessed to be able to mentor and influence the lives of numerous young people. One of the best things we can do is to pour into the lives of the next generation, to be able to mold and lead them. To be able show them by example.

As a Judge and a mother, I know the importance of inspiring and uplifting our young people. In these turbulent times, we must be the rock, the pillar the soft place to land. Our world today is so full of hate, racism and evil. We must be the light. We must walk in faith. We must share God with the next generation. We must raise them to be responsible, loving and teach them to love and to trust God.

I know I have been through a lot and I have walked my own journey. But I know God's plan is for me to use all I have gone through to teach and reach others. Each of us has a story and a gift to share with this world. And there is someone out there waiting on you to share yours.

Our world needs more Women of God to speak up! To make a difference and step into our roles as mentors and leaders. We are needed! We must listen to God and follow his will! I hope my story has inspired you and encouraged you. I pray it has given you strength and guidance.

<u>WORDS OF ENCOURAGEMENT</u>

If I could speak to the world, I would tell them learn to trust and love God. Love God first and love yourself! Don't let anyone disrespect you.

Always treat yourself like a Queen because you are a Queen! Know your worth. And don't let other people's inability to see your worth, change your value of yourself.

God gives us faith, but faith without works is dead! It tells us this in the bible. So, work hard for your dreams and your goals. Only you can make it happen. Push yourself hard toward your goals, anything worth having is going to take hard work. So, roll up your sleeves and put in the work, you will not regret.

Invest in yourself and in your dreams. You can do anything if you are willing to work hard for it. All you must do is want it and be willing to make it happen. If it is in God's will, He will make a way. The best thing to do is to pray over your plans, goals and dreams then ask God to guide you and lead you. Listen for his Voice!

I pray you will take time to be in God's word and take time to tell him your plans and dreams. Also, Take time to seek counsel from Godly advisors.

ABOUT THE AUTHOR

Judge Maria T. Jackson earned a B. A. in Political Science in 1987 from the University of Texas at Arlington (with honors) and a Doctor of Jurisprudence from Texas A & M University formerly known as Texas Wesleyan University School of Law. She is also a certified mediator. Judge Jackson has been the presiding Judge of the 339th State District court in Houston, Harris County, Texas since 2008. She was reelected November 8th, 2016 now serving her third term. Judge Jackson presides over serious felony offenses which run the gamut from low-level drug offenses to capital murder. She has presided over many jury trials and several have been featured nationally.

She is married to her soul mate Mr. Frank Jackson Hayes and together they share a beautiful harmonious family of 4 boys. Jackson, Blair, Tyler and Joshua. To learn more about the author please visit her website judgemariatjackson.com.

CHAPTER 37

TRUMP FAITH

Ce Ce Ferrari, California, USA

MY FAITH WAS TESTED

The day was June 15, 2015. Donald J. Trump rode down the escalator inside Trump Towers to announce his presidential bid for 2016. As I watched him glide down the escalator with his beautiful, gracious wife Melania by his side, I heard a voice within me that I had learned to trust. I call this voice Thunder. Thunder said to me, "Donald J. Trump will win the 2016 presidential election."

I am not religious. I am a mystic. I am inspired by voices and beings that are from the spiritual realm that come from sources of truth that enable me and others to transform. Spirituality is the fuel that moves and ignite people, places and situations. Some call Thunder, God, Lord, Universe, and the Great Spirit. When Thunder speaks—I listen! Before Trump walked off the escalator I was crying because the powerful vibration of Thunder's words sent chills throughout my body.

Many people laughed at me and told me I was crazy to entertain the possibility of a playboy, cocky, arrogant, billionaire becoming president of the United States of America.

Our country is in trouble and I knew God/Universe works in mysterious ways sometimes to create necessary change. The politically correct police had silenced expression of thought. Trump's bold, blunt, unfiltered style of communicating forced the politically correct police to take a seat. In God's time, we get what we need…not what we want.

After Trump publicly said Mexico wasn't sending their best and they were sending criminals and rapists, I was treated like a leper because I voiced he'd still make a good president. He didn't speak his words eloquently however I knew what he meant. There are many good Mexicans however illegal immigration has made conditions in poor black communities and many poor communities worse—not better.

GOD REVIVED ME AND REVEALED MY FAITH

Many political polls showed Trump had no chance of winning the presidency. During my mediations, Thunder often reminded me that Trump would be president. I was told to write a book about Trump and the title was given to me. I followed my spiritual counsel and I wrote the book, *TRUMP…Divine Intervention or Not?* with the sub-title: How Today's political shakeup is forcing all Americans to see their own hypocrisy.

I was told to put a picture of the White House on the book cover. Publishing experts told me it wouldn't be smart to put an image of the White House on the cover of the book because Trump hadn't won the election yet. I knew they were laughing at me because they didn't believe he had a chance of winning.

Through the election, I got closer to a powerful, God vibration and I trusted the messages that were given to me. In the past I rarely used the word God, however I found myself saying the word God often because

I was told it was God speaking to me. In the past I preferred saying the word Universe because I am turned off by the behavior of many religious people. I began to get comfortable with saying to others what God spoke to me about Trump. God said, "Trump is a sheep wearing wolves clothing. He has a good heart. He has been chosen."

Many times, during the election Trump said things that would've sank the possibility for most to get elected. Though Trump had low poll numbers I trusted and published the book before the election with the title and picture that was given to me during my meditation. Some people were appalled that I would use the word "Divine" when speaking about Trump. He is probably the least racist politician and I feel he's one of the most authentic.

People often say, "I don't discuss politics and religion." I learn a lot about people personally based on their willingness to discuss any topic and how they express themselves. Some think it's wise to avoid speaking about religion and politics. If we are emotionally mature and emotionally intelligent we should be able to discuss any subject. Someone said to me, "You won't change how I feel about politics and I won't change your mind. We can just agree to disagree." My purpose in discussing politics isn't to be right, but rather to have an understanding why people feel the way they do and to learn. Understanding melts fear and anger.

God has given me grace through this election and I have become a better listener and I can feel, see and hear the hypocrisy louder in myself and others.

MY FAITH WALK TODAY!

When it was announced that Donald J. Trump would be the 45th United States President, I screamed and cried, "Lord, you told me! You told me!" I made a vow to trust Thunder's voice more than ever. Trump will make a good president; however, he can't make America greater by himself. He needs all of us.

I was told in another meditation to start a letter campaign to President Trump. The campaign is called: My Letter to Trump. The letters I am encouraging people to write to him aren't only about asking him what he can do for you and your community but rather it's about what YOU can and are willing to do to be a part of making America greater.

Trump isn't perfect and at times he's rough around the edges however we are blessed to have a president who is proud to be an American, wants to improve the lives of veterans and who says, "Americans first." I believe him when he says he wants to help improve conditions in black inner cities. It will take more than Trump's desire to make this happen. This can be done if black people truly believe "Black Lives Matter" by treating each other with dignity and respect.

It has been interesting to see many Christians who claim they trust everything happens in God's time have a difficult time accepting Trump is the new president.

Because of this election, and because I am a black woman, I am more eager than ever to be a powerful voice in the black community to help lift people's spirits' who don't feel they have value and self-worth because they have become victim's and have bought into the belief that racist white men are stopping them from becoming and being their best selves. I want to help poor people be able to reach inside of themselves and touch the greatness that they were born with by changing their poor habits to productive habits.

WORDS OF ENCOURAGEMENT

I have experienced the worst discrimination ever because I am a Trump supporter. Hypocrisy is at an all-time high! People who say they don't like Trump because he discriminates have discriminated against me by refusing to work on my website, books and do marketing for me.

Unlike many, I am excited about the anger, hate and rage that's happening in America because it's a gift that it's been uprooted for us to heal.

The election is just a symptom of negative emotions that have been repressed for many decades. We won't heal unless we all see our role by having self-awareness and self-analysis. The angriest and the most hateful people only see flaws in others and they choose to be blinded and not see that like all humans they too are racists, hypocrites, sexist, bias and liars.

Family is supposed to be the most important thing, however if this was true people we claim to love would feel free to express how they feel even when their beliefs differ. We aren't loving people when we tell them they aren't allowed to discuss politics or any other subject with us. This is a form of control and often stems from a need to be right. Open honest communication is love. When we truly love people, we don't put muzzles on their mouths and self-expression.

I challenge you to see God, spirituality and yourself in every person and situation and surrender to what is. See where you are being that which you complain about. Ask yourself, "What can I do to make America greater?"

What you resist will persist.

ABOUT THE AUTHOR

Ce Ce Ferrari is a Transformational—Mystic Vangelist Speaker and Author. She's an expert at helping people become emotionally mature and emotionally intelligent by connecting with their hidden emotions.

She's a former Miami Metro Dade Police Officer and Mega-Watt radio personality. She lives in Southern California. She's writing her next book, *My Letters to Trump*. To hire Ce Ce for speaking engagements and to find out My Letters to Trump campaign, new book releases, blog and newsletters, visit: CeCeFerrari.com

XVIII.

TESTIMONY IN FAITH

CHAPTER 38

THE HOLIDAY THAT CHANGED MY LIFE

Placida Acheru

United Kingdom

"TRUST ME I HAVE GOT YOUR BACK", SAYS THE LORD

The 8th September 1983 is a day I will never forget. I had accepted an invitation to spend my holiday with my godmother. I did not know that it would have such an impact on my life. The visit changed everything for me and was the beginning of my Christian journey.

Every aspect of that day is clearly written into my memory. I skipped into the dining room looking forward to hugging my Godmother, to find not my Godmother but one of her relations sharing the gospel with my godmother's daughter. They invited me to sit and listen. As I absorbed the lessons of the gospel, I was inspired by every word I heard. It was explained to me that these stories I was hearing were the Words of God. I knew from that moment that these were to words by which I wanted to live my life. That was the day I gave my life to Christ.

When I arrived back home, I felt like I was the first to bring the good news of God into my family. I had been brought up a Christian, but the message had somehow missed me. The love of God impacted the way I saw the world. His light was so bright, everything looked beautiful. I could not describe this love, except that I was literally renewed. Reborn if you like. Everything was good and nothing could go wrong. I was in my teens and with my new passion, I shared my new faith to any and every one that would listen.

My faith grew stronger as I joined a Christian group and started to discuss religion with my new friends. The church I found was very strict on its teaching and preached repent or perish. The women were bonded by very conservative dressing rules. It was not an easy time in my home as my parents could not understand why I had chosen to join "the frustrated" peoples group as they called it.

An aunt from my father's family called me aside one day and told me, "Placida the people who become born-again, well they do not get married! Do you want to be an old maid"?

The more I was cautioned the more I went head deep into my Christian activities. I would leave school for camps and join campus crusade. Life was good. I had no complaints and no one could convince me I was on the wrong path.

WE ARE ONE AND WE MUST LOVE ONE ANOTHER

As I learnt more about the larger Christian community, I began to discover that praying and following the right path can come in an infinite number of interpretations. Different Christian groups teach different types of behavioral practices to prove your love of God. As fervent as we were in the group I belonged, I found it difficult to believe that another Christian group would describe my group as none Christian. Yet, my sect also considered other groups less committed than us.

People stayed within their circles and did not mix for fear of being less Christian by their adopted group. Not very Christian I know.

One day I saw a friend reading a book with an appealing title. Bannered across the front cover was the words "The Happiest People on Earth" …. (you can find the link for the book at the end my article together with other useful references).

Within the book, I discovered there was a group called "Full Gospel Business Men Fellowship". The story of how this group was started was so inspiring, the people within the pages sounded so loving and friendly. They were truly living my interpretation of a life dedicated to Christ.

I could not contain the excitement of my new discovery, so shared the story of this book my friends. I discovered that the Full Gospel Business Men Fellowship was already operating in my city.

Enquiring more, I found the date and time of the next meeting. I recall the occasion of my first meeting very well even, to my surprise being the only student in the room. The meeting was held in a beautiful hotel venue. It felt like the pages of the book had come alive. The atmosphere was different, there was love and joy and peace. And yes, they were happy. They were truly the happiest people I had met on earth.

Something struck me, as I observed the meeting, it was the women. The women were dressed wrong. How are they able to be in the spirit, wearing makeup and trousers? Why do they have their hair open.? I pondered to myself. In my student, Christian group, these people would be categorized as sinners and not worthy to follow the path of God. They had no right to be happy.

My lesson that day was that "we are one and we must love one another". As I went back to school, and prayed, the bible passage in Luke chapter 6 became alive.

"Do not judge, and you will not be judged. Do not condemn, and you will not be condemned. Forgive, and you will be forgiven. Give, and it will be given to you. A good measure, pressed down, shaken together and running over, will be poured into your lap. For with the measure you use, it will be measured to you." He also told them this parable: "Can the blind lead the blind? Will they not both fall into a pit? The student is not above the teacher, but everyone who is fully trained will be like their teacher. "Why do you look at the speck of sawdust in your brother's eye and pay no attention to the plank in your own eye? How can you say to your brother, 'Brother, let me take the speck out of your eye,' when you yourself fail to see the plank in your own eye? You hypocrite, first take the plank out of your eye, and then you will see clearly to remove the speck from your brother's eye".
Luke 6: 37-42 (NIV)

I could crown my prayer with these simple words "God, make me the Placida you want me to be".

THE POTTER'S CLAY

Life continued to improve. It felt good to have no sins or troubles. I was the perfect Christian with a perfect life. I remember in a small gathering of young students who were from a similar family class. One said. "We have no sins, we all got born-again at very young age and are faithful". It felt like we are perfect for the mission to go out into the world and preach the gospel.

Looking back, it seems that statement opened a can of worms. Each one of us began to experience big emotional shifts in our lives. A test of our faith; life began to test us and teach us.

For me, it started with my parents splitting up and the stable secure good life I led began to fizzle away. With my father gone, my mother, me and my three younger siblings went from plenty to nothing in no time at all. Having never known need, now getting a meal each day became a problem.

I wanted to find a husband, but I could not make relationships last. When I did eventually, joy only lasted 3 months and this Christian girl found herself in a divorce.

This incidence shook my faith. I could not understand what had gone wrong and what I had done to make this happen. I was sure I prayed, I was very sure God said yes, my pastor and all my Christian family, agreed that this union was from God.

If this is so, how come it was over?

What had I done to deserve a broken heart?

I know had the stigma of a failed married against my name too! It was not a straight forward separation. Families got involved. Emotions were high. Blame was attributed. Acceptance was slow.

I waited, prayed, fasted and doing everything I was told to do by God. Time past and on the seventh year after my married the divorce was finalized.

There were nights of pain and tears. It took me a while to understand that I was being passed through the furnace and being prepared for a future where I would use my story to heal and improve the lives of others.

I felt like Job, God seemed so far fetch.

Job 23: 8-10 *"Behold, I go forward, but he is not there; and backward, but I cannot perceive him: On the left hand, where he doth work, but I cannot behold him: he hideth himself on the right hand, that I cannot see him: But he knoweth the way that I take: when he hath tried me, I shall come forth as gold". (KJV)*

Gods way is not our way. He uses the imperfect and when uncertainty over shadows, the darkness is too deep, that is when HE decides to get involved. He tests our faith!

God's word never promised a life of no stress. I know this now. Think of all the people that died and suffered persecution in his name. The making of a beautiful clay pot pounding and beating, the result is beautiful and so is the making of gold. Today I understand that the journey was necessary to bring me to a better place.

THE POWER OF VISIONS

A visit to the UK was necessary, I wanted space to think and discover what's next. That visit led me to the discovery of a new career. I have always helped people, I like to see others progress, I never knew that what I did had a name – Coaching. Yes! I discovered coaching, another light bulb moment. I had found me; this is what I am called to do and be.

Life in the UK was not quite smooth. It took a while finding my place in a new country and still seeking to understand what life holds for me. In one of my training courses as an entrepreneur, a friend shared with me a story. The passion and belief radiating from her as she shared the path taken was intoxicating. It was not that her story sounded too good to be true. I could see the evidence of her success. What was amazing was the path she had taken from a dark place to reach where she was now.

The path we take is complicated and complex, intertwining with other people's journeys. It was not until later that I realized my involvement in her success. As she told me her story, it did not occur to me that it could also work for me. I did not understand the principles. I did not know it was a natural law that would work for everyone if they requested it completely.

Some years later, I was in a rut. We all know this feeling. Our vision is unclear; our options seem limited; I felt it was my struggle and that no one was going to throw me a life line. I was in a deep pit, with no options for escape. I was in a dark place. I was all alone. I saw a glimmer of light. A thought. I remember my friend's story and her journey out of the dark. I went back to my friend to find out more about that "vision board" thing.

My Vision Board was already evidencing itself in my life. My friend was right. It is a natural law. Why then do we remain unaware of this relationship with your life outcomes? It happens so often. Can you guess what she said when I got in contact with her?

"Excellent timing", she said "there is a workshop in 2 days starting soon and there is one place left". I do not need to be asked twice. I signed up immediately.

I left the workshop a different person. My view of life had changed. My vision board became my frequent habit and my belief. I had created boards for the different areas of my life. A lot of the content on my first and second board has manifested itself in even better ways than I would ever have imagined. If you saw my smile, you would know I speak the truth. I could see a clear picture of what I want in life,

I must tell you that, I was sceptic at first, I hoped this is not in conflict with my faith as a Christian. I do not want to dabble in anything ungodly. As I prayed for guidance, scriptures were revealed to me.

I began to understand some of the more important teachings:

"The LORD said to Abram, ""Look around from where you are, to the north and south, to the east and west. All the land that you see I will give to you and your offspring forever."Gen13: 14-15 (NIV)

Then another scripture jumped out at me, it was the story about Jacob and his father in-law.

"And Jacob took him rods of green poplar, and of the hazel and chestnut tree; and pilled white strakes in them, and made the white appear which was in the rods. And he set the rods which he had pilled before the flocks in the gutters in the watering troughs when the flocks came to drink, that they should conceive when they came to drink. And the flocks conceived before the rods, and brought forth cattle ringstraked, speckled, and spotted. And Jacob did separate the lambs, and set the faces of the flocks toward the ringstraked, and all the brown in the flock of Laban; and he put his own flocks by themselves, and put them not unto Laban's cattle."
Gen 30: 37-40 (KJV)

What does this mean?

And then another scripture came to me.

"Finally, brethren, whatsoever things are true, whatsoever things are honest, whatsoever things are just, whatsoever things are pure, whatsoever things are lovely, whatsoever things are of good report; if there be any virtue, and if there be any praise, think on these things." – Philippians 4:8(NIV)

I began to apply more of the scripture in my life. The more I focused on the things that are good, pure, holy and removed my mind from the weight of my past hurt began to lift.

My business picked up and relationships with friends and family got better. It was all there in the scriptures, all I needed was to move my mind from the negative and focus on the positive. Just like Abraham, let my vision go as far as I can see and allow God to do his thing.

When things were bad and relationships were not working, I kept remembering what my aunt said to me. "You are going to be an old maid because you have chosen the path of Christ". I would have been, if I continued to focus on her words and all the things that had happened to me in the past. I praise God for the man in my life, he is God sent and I mean it in every sense.

This new revelation, felt like a magic wand. Again, I shared with friends who were facing hard times and when they focused on the positive things began to shift for them.

I could not keep my discovery to myself, so I decided to share it with more people by running a workshop. I was not sure how this would be received by my delegates, but to my surprise the event was very successful. The Vision Activation Workshop was born. More and more people have benefited from the teaching I share and its attendance continues to grow. If you would like to know more about the workshop you can learn more at http://placidaacheru.com/visionactivation

Till this day, I can see why as Christians we remove our eyes from the things that are not pure and holy. The news is filled with negativity and so we attract more of what we do not want.

Gods promises offers us the good things of life.

In conclusion, life will imprint its mark on us, what we do with it is up to us. Our journey is not for us to keep to ourselves but to use and help others to stand. And so, I encourage you as you read these lines to ask God, who and what HE wants you to be, then focus on just that. Remember HE has your back. Selah.

ABOUT THE AUTHOR

Placida Acheru, founder of Unleashed Women's Network and Coaching4Excellence, is a top UK Business Transformation Coach, 3x International Bestselling Author, Coach and Mentor. She is dedicated to guiding others toward taking charge of their lives; breaking through roadblocks to systematically transform their everyday into the power to create wealth.

She has empowered thousands of business owners across the globe to become independent, gain visibility, credibility, and increasing their list by over 250% generating consistent streams of income.

Placida inspires her audience through her signature events

http://womanunleashyourpotential.com
and http://visionactivationworkshop.com

Connect with Placida:

Website: http://placidaacheru.com/start
Facebook Business: http://placidaacheru.com/Facebook
Twitter: https://twitter.com/Placida_Acheru
Instagram: https://www.instagram.com/placida_acheru/
Link to the book: "The Happiest People on Earth" http://amzn.to/2gb9bgU

CHAPTER 39

SPIRITUAL TESTIMONY

Fiona Pearce, Adelaide, Australia

My name is Fiona. I was born in Victoria but I was raised in Adelaide. I grew up in the Seventh Day Adventist Church.

MY FAITH WAS TESTED

When reached my early 30's I started struggling with a lot of personal issues which I couldn't understand at the time and in some ways, they are still some things I don't understand about my experiences.

When I was 36, I was single, living at home and unemployed. These a couple of reasons I have been struggling with depression for the last few years. I always thought that I would be working, married and have a couple of kids by now. A lot of my friends who were my age were working, married and starting their own families. I felt so left out and alone. It was like everybody's life was moving forward but mine was just staying where it has always been.

I was 32 turning 33 that my depression was at my worse and I have since had many ups and downs to the same reasons. I struggled to keep my head above water. It felt like there was this massive war that was going on in my head; one side was telling me that I am good enough, I will get a job, get married, have kids, etc. Then the other side was telling me that I will never find a job, no one will ever love me, live at home for the rest of my life, no kids as I would be too old. Unfortunately, the side that was telling me all the latter was winning and I went in to a deep, dark depression.

It all started when I told a guy that I was interested in him and he didn't return my feelings. So, I felt hurt, rejected and abandoned something which I had felt my whole life. It was the first time that I felt I could open in anyway especially to a man which I had never done before. I don't trust men easily. My father left when I was 18 months old so I never really knew how to trust a man. This was the first time that I every really let my guard down to let someone in like that. I know that it may seem like these issues I am dealing with may be trivial and not a major disaster. Then I started thinking about it and what God says about us. We are all God's children and God know what we are feeling and what we are going through. He feels our pain, we hurt God hurts, when we cry, God cries. So, for that reason why should I trivialize what I am going through just because someone might not understand?

I did a course in January 2011 and there was something that the trainer told us that I will always remember which is what helped me to be able to do what I needed to get the help I really needed to put myself out of the dark. So, this is what we were told in that course that helped me through the worse period of my life; 'Being on stage is the most powerful but also the most vulnerable position to be in'. So, I took all the vulnerability I was feeling and turned it into the most powerful position to be in. I took a chance, went to my GP to ask for help so I asked for a referral to a psychologist so I could get the help I needed. I needed to take control of what I was thinking and feeling and trust myself again.

So, in some ways tried to throw myself in to everything and anything to get my end of things and to forget what I was feeling and feel like everything was ok, like I was ok. I tried to keep myself busy so that about how hurt and depressed I was.

It was because of this that I eventually stopped going to church, (there were also other issues involved), but I didn't want anyone to see me as I didn't want anyone to know that I was suffering so in the most part I suffered in silence as even my family didn't know what was going on. All I wanted to do was hide so one could see 'the real me' or that is what I thought was the real me.

However, I knew I couldn't cut God out of my life and I never would so I did do a lot of praying and asking God to help me and to also have the strength to forgive this guy and to forgive myself so read may inspirational devotions this helped me as I knew I wasn't alone. I also read little devotions that gave some comfort and had some bible texts that made things seem not so bad. Some of these inspirational quotes were what helped me through as the words I was reading somehow helped. One passage that I read a lot was about Comfort in Rejection; passage was very easy to understand as at the time I was so down and felt like there was no way out of what I was feeling and this helped me to realize that there is a light at the end of the tunnel.

This passage read: '*Putting yourself 'out there' with another person is when you offer your friendship or even your heart to someone. There is no doubt that it's a vulnerable position to be in. Hopefully, your friendship or love is returned, but this is not always the case.*

Rejection is painful and can bruise your self-image. What do you do when you've offered your heart to someone who turns and walks away? How do you find comfort?

There is no denying that rejection hurts or that Satan will use the experience of rejection to try and sink you even deeper into depression.

Your only hope of recovery is to focus your mind on positive things. Focus on the people in your life who love you. Focus on God's promise to always be with you. Focus on your worth in God's eyes.

Just because one person walks away from you does not mean everyone else will to.'

There are some beautiful Bible verses that a little quote and prayer that go with this passage which was also very comforting to me at the worse time of my life.

The first text is Deuteronomy 31:8 *The Lord Himself goes before you and will be with you; He will never leave you or forsake you. Do not be afraid; do not be discouraged.*

The second text is 1 Samuel 12:22 *For the sake of His great name the Lord will not reject His people, because the Lord was pleased to make you his own.*

The quote, which is anonymous was something that I really needed at the time as it made me realize that what I was feeling and what I went through was real and not just something that happens.

The quote is *"Giving someone all you love is never an assurance that they'll love you back. Don't expect love in return just wait for it to grow in their hearts, but if it doesn't, be content it grew in mine."*

This is a prayer that became a lifeline... *'Dear Father, please remind me how much I mean to You. It's hard to focus on that when my heart is hurting so much. Thank you for Your Word that tells me I matter to you. Thank you for the comfort of Your love. Help me to look forward to tomorrow instead of focusing on the pain of today. Amen.'* (from the book, Daily Inspirations of Comfort)

Another passage which is from the same book is about 'Comfort is Love'. This passage is as follows: *'Knowing you are loved is just about the best thing in the world. A real security comes with love that means you can trust the other person to stick with you, regardless of what happens. Love gives you the courage to be yourself, confidence to try new things and energy to involve other people in your life.*

Love gives you the strength to face whatever life throws at you. Being loved by others is certainly wonderful.

But the best love of all is God's love. His love is constant and steady. It has no strings attached. It is forgiving. God's love is pure and makes all the other love possible.

Accepting God's love for you and understand how valuable you are to Him lays a groundwork for accepting love from another person. It also gives you the freedom and ability to love another person. Thank God for His love.'

This passage always reminds me of the verse in '*1 Corinthians 13:13 And now these three remain: faith, hope and love. But the greatest of these is love.'*

This is so true in so many ways. But it is also something that gets lost in everyday life, especially when you are struggling to find out where you fit in life but there is always something that will never change; I am God's child, God's love for me will never fail, falter, or die. God's love for me will be never ending.

There are two texts that go with this passage which also give strength and courage. One is Romans 5:5 '*Hope does not disappoint us, because God has poured out His love into our hearts by the Holy Spirit, whom He has given us.'*

The second text is; 1 John 4:12 '*No one has ever seen God; but if we love one another, God lives in us and His love is made complete in us.'*

As the quote says by Leighton Ford '*God loves us the way we are, but too much to leave us that way'*

The prayer that follows is: Dear Father, I am constantly amazed by your love. It is amazing. Your loves make me more loving to those around me. Thank you for Your incredible model of love. Let You love shine through me to all those in my life. Amen.'
(from the book, Daily Inspirations of Comfort)

I love Christmas time as it is one of, well actually the most amazing time of year. I love what the Christmas Season means. It is one of my favorite times of year and sometimes I don't think one day is enough.

I love the time as there are trees, tinsel, bells, glitter, baubles, toys, ribbons, and many, many more special Christmas spirit.

Although, Christmas is one of my favorite times of year it is also a little sad as I do feel alone. I am single, living at home, was unemployed and very broke. However, one of the things that I love about Christmas is the joys of the season as you don't need to spend great amounts of money or buy the biggest present. It is about what is in your heart. I have always believed that anything be it Christmas, Easter, birthdays or any occasion is what you make it. That is why I always try and enjoy it. Christmas time is about being with the people you love and enjoying what God gave us in the way of family and friends and not worrying about what we don't have but the love and joy we get in being together as friends and family. The true blessing of Christmas is that Christ was born. That is the best gift of all.

In October, last year I was lucky enough to get a job. It was a 6-month Government contract and it finished on 1 April 2016. I hoped that this would help to lead to other jobs but that has not yet happened. It is now the end of October 2016 and I still haven't found another job. It is starting to get to me as it is making me second guess myself and my worth.

When I was working, I saw a guy who you could basically say had me at hello. However, as I found out (by accident) he does have a girlfriend who also worked at the same place. Even though this was disappointing and upsetting I also didn't make the same mistake I did before by telling him.

I am now 38 and I have no idea what is install for my life. My biggest fear is that I will never find someone, love someone, get married, have children. That somehow scares me more than not finding a job. God never intended for human to be solo creatures. That is why he created Adam and Eve rather than just create one person and then just gradually add people to the planet one at time. We are not meant to be alone, he created this world for us to share and enjoy.

The one thing that I would like to know when I leave this world is that I have left a part of me behind in the way of my Children knowing that they will be a part of me and that I will always be a part of them as they continue grow and make their own families and life. That is what I want my legacy to be, so I will always be remembered.

I know that God has a plan for my life, I just don't know what that is. I know that with God anything is possible.

Even though I still have not gone back to Church I still have my faith. Sometimes I believe that this faith is the only thing that is getting me through so many things. I do miss the people that are at the church as I have grown up with them in my life since I was 5. Some of them are more like family then friends. I truly believe that I was lead to this Church for that reason. That this church would become my extended family.

Even though I have and will always have my heavenly father, I believe that I was given an earthly surrogate father who is and will always be a father to me which is why I ended up growing up in this Church and I hope one will walk me down the aisle for my wedding. Which I know will happen one day.

All I can do is pray: '*Dear Father, sometimes I am afraid... very afraid. I am thankful to know that you are with me. I'm glad I'm not alone... but I'm still afraid. Help me to trust you with the situation, to depend on You for protection. Comfort me in my fear. Amen.*' (from the book, Daily Inspirations of Comfort)

While the thought of getting older does scare me as the older I get the less likely my dream of having children gets further away. However, despite that I like to still celebrate my birthday as I like to enjoy the friends and family I do have and are important to me rather than focus on the things I don't have. God is leading my life... I just don't know where... But I know that God will never leave me, no matter where life takes me in that sense I will never be alone, He is my Rock.

Now I have my learner's I feel like I have a direction (no pun intended). But I know that there will be a job that will come up soon, who knows maybe that will be my Christmas present this year.

There will always be times when I feel vulnerable and scared but I know that I can have the power to be who I want to be. God's love will always be there as a light to lead me through what appears to be the darkest days that I have yet to face. Even though it has been 5 years since my depression was at its worst (even though I think it was always there but due to the circumstances it pushed me over in to the pit of depression). There will always be good and bad days and there are times that I need reminding of the strength that God has given me to get through this. Although, I will do whatever it takes to fight and not give up on what is important to me.

I know my dreams will come true and that is worth believing in and fighting for. I want my dream life to come true and I know that it will happen. I will have a life, move out of home, have my own family, and find a job which will also be a career. I am me and I am proud of who I am. God loves me for who I am.

I will keep praying for God to lead me and show me the way... I still have a long journey ahead and I trust that I will eventually understand why my life has turned out this way. I have a long way to go and there is so much more I must offer in life. So many things to do, so many experiences to explore and so many more people to meet.

I pray... '*Dear Father, you are my lifeline. You are what pulls me from the pit of depression. Thank you for being my anchor. Help me to focus my thoughts on You and not on those things that will drag me back into the pit. Amen.*' (from the book,

Daily Inspirations of Comfort)

I will keep praying that you will lead me in the right direction as I know you will never give up on me...

Thank you for loving me for who I am and accepting me for the person I will be.

XIX.

FATHER'S &
DAUGHTER'S

CHAPTER 40

GOD IS MY GUIDE

Sol Macias, TX, USA

MY FAITH WAS TESTED

M y father was a strong-willed man. With only a third-grade education and the clothes on his back he immigrated to the United States to be able to offer his children a better life. He led our family with intense commitment and fury. It was clear, the responsibility of his household was his, and his alone. He ignored his own pain and suffering to create a concrete base for his family. His mission in life never wavered and he continued to lead until the last moment of his death. Both my mother and father were staying with me a few weeks to help me with the care of my newborn daughter. I had not found a decent daycare to place her in and they agreed to help until I found placement. They traveled hundreds of miles and put their life on hold for me. This was such a common action from them that I never realized my ungratefulness.

The Sunday that I lost my father started off very normal. Both my father and mother loved to attend flea markets and shop. My father began to have chest pain while at the market and went inside a bathroom. My mom, not recognizing the symptoms, didn't think anything of it and continued without him. A few minutes later my father collapsed on the ground. He had chest pain and couldn't breathe. He was loaded onto an ambulance and he was gone before he made it to the hospital. In a matter of hours my life changed forever.

The pain of losing a loved one coupled with the pain of having to lose them so quickly brought me to my knees. I was not physically, emotionally, or spiritually prepared for such a quick and tragic loss. My world broke that day. Everything I thought I knew about strength and resiliency broke into a million pieces. With it went my faith. The big question of "why" suffocated me. All the struggles in my life floated to the top completely blocking any logical thinking. I thought about being bullied at school as a child and how I used to pray every night that it would stop, and it never did. I thought about the death of my 16-month old niece passing away from a simple cold because we could not afford proper medical care.

I thought about going away for college and struggling with depression alone. I remembered all the times that I cried out to him with no response. I concluded that God did not love me because he had continuously made me struggle without being able to understand "why." This was the last time I would pray to him and request assistance. My faith broke that day and every day after that felt like I was drowning.

My life became a rollercoaster of emotions. One day there was peace the next there was rage. One moment I loved the next second I hated everyone, including myself. It was a never-ending cycle of extreme feelings and emotions that would lead me into some very dark places.

GOD REVIVED ME & REVEALED MY FAITH

It wasn't so long ago that my life sunk into deep waters hitting the bottom of a dark dead ocean. I remember feeling sick. A paralyzing sickness overtook my body. I realized there was nothing left to give. There was no good or bad in me, there was just sickness. This was what is known as "rock bottom." I knew I was there because I felt it. That place was cold, dark, and painful. My days were filled with people, but I felt completely alone. I continued to go on with everyday things, trying to burry everything I felt. I could not make decisions and when I did I second guessed those decisions. I walked and didn't trust my own steps. Essentially, I had lost my purpose. I didn't know what direction I was going in. When I laid my head down at night it spun out of control causing many sleepless nights.

One day I decided to ask God the same question I have been asking him for years, "why". I wasn't expecting a response. I didn't receive a response. Instead I felt a feeling in my heart growing. A feeling of kindness, compassion, and empathy for myself. I was so used to helping and serving others. I was used to taking care of others as a mother, a wife, and a police officer. I was not used to taking care of me. As I tuned into that feeling in my heart I started to have many ideas on different ways that I could care for myself. I started to take time off and spent it in bed reading or resting. I told myself it was ok to take time out of the day to acknowledge my accomplishments. I accepted the fact that I was not perfect. I forgave myself for past decisions that had brought me pain. I stood in the mirror and told that person that she was loved no matter what. I began to believe that I was worth it. I began to believe that I was important. I began to believe that I had worth and that I deserved to be forgiven.

Once I accepted that I deserved to be forgiven my heart filled with dignity. That dignity gave me strength and courage. I now had the strength and conviction to carry me dreams into the realm of reality. It cleared all the mental blocks I had about myself allowing my dreams to expand,

and I was finally able to visualize them. I was finally able to visualize myself, the true me, flaws and all. I saw the kindness, the compassion, and the beauty God had blessed me with since birth. I now had the courage to embrace him and myself. Essentially, God revived and revealed faith to me through self -love and forgiveness.

MY FAITH WALK TODAY

Every day is a struggle to show self-love. It is not an easy road when you have spent most of your life doubting, underestimating, or hating yourself. The first step for me was tuning into God's message in my heart. The second step was trusting his message and acting on it. I didn't know it back then, but that feeling that I got in the bottom of that dark abyss was HIM. He had never left me. I was listening, but not feeling. The third step was letting go of my need to control. Sometimes we are under the impression most of the things happen because you push and you make them happen. Yes and no. The other part of the equation is if you push too much and too fast you will not reach your destination, and you will pass it up. I found that my journey should be challenging, but not painful. I found that when I move to fast I lose purpose. I lose that feeling in my heart that guides me. I lose HIS voice.

Forgiveness has not come easy either. To accept the "wrong" you have done is to accept that you are flawed. To accept that you are flawed is to accept that you are not perfect and that your life will continuously be a struggle. HE is the only one that can bring piece. Forgiveness was finding piece in me that allowed me to grow and change at his calling not on mine. All the frustration and pain that I had put myself through was because I was not ready and I had impatiently pushed at the wrong time. That constant movement to achieve, to grow, to learn, and to be was destroying me. To stop the self-destruction, I had to tune in to HIS love and to receive his message I had to love and forgive myself.

There are days where those self-defeating voices begin whispering in my ear. I know them too well. They come when I feel discouraged, defeated, sad, lonely, tired, and angry. I center myself and reach into my heart for compassion. I remind myself that kindness and compassion are not only for the people around me, but for myself. This is the only way that I can silence those self-defeating voices. As I become stronger in my faith and I will one day can silence them forever.

Growing up I was never taught to take care of myself or how to love myself. Instead, I was taught to take care of others first because this showed sacrifice, and God loved those who sacrificed for others. Through the years of "sacrifice" I became weak and when tragedy hit I broke. Everything came tumbling down. I found myself in situations that I had walked into on my own because I had lost it all. Nevertheless, HE never left my side and I finally slowed down and felt his love.

There are no magic cures. Every day is a new day. Struggle is constant and therefore, it is a constant arrangement of thoughts. There is a constant fight for peace and silence. I am constantly trying to tune myself into HIS love. There are times when the voices win, but I recognize when I walk up to this edge. I know what it feels to be one step away. No matter what, I go into a quiet space wherever I may find myself and I pray until I love myself and God. I bring myself back and begin again. It doesn't matter how many times I must repeat. I know what lies at the edge and I don't want to be there. There are times when I fall and HE is always there to catch me. I picks me up, he dusts me off, and he holds me until I can walk and begin again.

I have finally embraced this constant struggle to survive in a world filled with drop offs. I am not counting the times I fall off because HE is not counting the times he picks me up. I know he will be there for me eternally. All I need to do is call on HIM and feel his presence and love. All I must do is allow HIM to love me. His love will allow me the courage to have compassion and kindness for myself. There is no easy way. It is a constant fight to love myself, it is a constant fight to feel HIM.

WORDS OF ENCOURAGEMENT

There is no other way but trusting in HIM. God will always be by my side. I know I will never walk alone. He will always pick me up when I fall. He will love me and help me heal. He will always forgive me and help me forgive myself. HIS love will give me the room that I need to heal and love again. Trust in HIM, and you will also feel the power of his love. The power of his love will speak to you as it did for me. It is not easy, but it can be accomplished daily. Once you have this down you can turn around and show someone else how to slow down, be still, and feel HIS love. This is how we can change the world one person at a time. We cannot keep HIM for ourselves. We must go out into the world and show others that HE is real, HE is the beginning, and HE is the answer.

As you go through your struggles remember that you are not alone. When you hit "rock bottom" remember this may be the time where stillness will dominate. Take this opportunity to feel what God is telling you. Allow yourself to feel HIS love. Allow HIM to lift you up and dust you off. Does this mean that you will not fall ever again? No. It means that you will understand that HE will always be there to comfort you when you fall. You must only be still and listen for HIS love. HIS love will allow you to heal, forgive, love, and move forward.

ABOUT THE AUTHOR

Off. Sol Macias is an 11 year Police Officer. She holds a bachelor in Spanish Literature from the University of Houston-DT and is currently pursuing a master in Criminal Justice from the University of Houston-DT

Off. Macias is the founder of Inspire Society a non-profit organization that connects law enforcement with the community through creative collaboration with other organizations, field work, and social media

Off. Macias Is the creator, author, and lead photographer of Latinamomninjadiaries.com where she writes police stories and motivational pieces for women in non-traditional career paths. Off. Macias is a member of various blogging networks that help her distribute her stories out on social media. Off. Macias is a first-time published author in an anthology focusing on Domestic Violence called Echoes in the Darkness. Off. Macias is also a speaker and has spoken at various schools educating parents, students, and teachers on the dangers of drugs, domestic violence, and sexual assault. She is currently founding a for profit media company, Sol Creative Media LLC.

Off. Macias belongs to various community organizations such as the National Hispanic Professional Association, Latin Women's Initiative, Houston Media Alliance, Pan-American Roundtable of Houston, Houston Hispanic Media Professionals Association, serves as the Vice Chair of Development at the Hispanic Women's Network of Texas, and serves as the secretary for the Organization of Spanish Speaking Officer's. Off. Macias has two children and she loves to read, write, and eat out.

You can reach Off. Macias at ninjadiaries@outlook.com and find her blog at latinamomninjadiaries.com.

BIBLIOGRAPHY

CBN. (n.d.). Forgiving Your Son's Killer | CBN.com. Retrieved from http://www1.cbn.com/video/forgiving-your-sonskiller

Columbia University Press. (2016). Locust facts, information, pictures | Encyclopedia.com articles about locust. In Encyclopedia.com | Free Online Encyclopedia (6th ed.). Retrieved from http://www.encyclope-dia.com/topic/locust.aspx

GotQuestions.org. (2016). What is Righteousness? Retrieved from http://www.gotquestions.org/righteousness.html

GotQuestions.org. (n.d.). How does God restore the years that the lo-custs have eaten (Joel 2:25)?

Retrieved September 19, 2016, from http://www.gotquestions.org/re-store-years-locustseaten.html

Hamel, J. (2016). Righteousness Right Standing with God. Retrieved from http://www.johnhamelministries.org/FBB_2_Right_Sta nding. htm

"Holy, Holy, Holy!" is a Christian hymn written by Reginald Heber (1783–1826). [1][2][3] Its lyrics speak specifically of the Holy Trinity, [2][3] having been written for use on Trinity Sunday. [3] It quotes the Sanctus of the Latin Mass, which translated into English begins "Holy, Holy, Holy! Lord God of Hosts". The text also paraphrases Revelation 4:1–11. John Bacchus Dykes composed the tune Nicaea for this hymn in 1861. [1][2][3] The tune name is a tribute to the First Council of Nicaea which formalized the doctrine of the Trinity in 325. [2][3]

REFRENCES & RESOURCES

o **24/7 Pill Addicts Hotline - Get Immediate Advice for Free 24/7.**

Ad · AmericanAddictionCenters.org/Pills

Get Immediate Advice **for** Free 24/7. Insurance May Cover 100%. Call Now!

Financial Information · Addiction Treatment · Insurance Verification

- Our Treatment Centers

- Admissions Process

- Our Quality Programs

- Payment Options

o **Military Sexual Assault | safehelpline.org**

Ad · www.safehelpline.org

Are you a sexual assault survivor in the military? Get help you deserve

RAINN, the nation's largest anti-sexual violence organization, ...

Mobile Site · Take A Tour · Get in Touch

- How to Get Help

- Transitioning Service Member

- DoD Safe Helpline

- Understanding Sexual Assault

- About RAINN

- Contact Us

o ## National Help Hotlines - Search for National Help Hotlines.

Ad · About.com/**National** Help **Hotlines** · About.com

Search **for National** Help **Hotlines**. Find Expert Advice on About.com.

o ## 24 Hour Anxiety Hotline - #1 Website for Online Therapy.

Ad · www.BetterHelp.com · Better Help

#1 Website **for** Online Therapy. Start Your Free Trial Today!

Convenient & Affordable · Discrete Counseling · Risk Free 7 Day Trial

1. Help hotlines | womenshealth.gov

https://**www.womenshealth.gov**/mental-health/**hotlines**

Help **hotlines**. Below is a list of **national** resources and **hotlines** that provide anonymous, confidential information to callers. They can answer questions and help you ...

2. National DV Hotline - Official Site

www.the**hotline**.org

Since 1996, the **National Domestic Violence Hotline** has been the vital link to safety **for women**, men, children and families affected by **domestic violence**.

o Get Help Today · Abuse Defined · What is Live Chat · Resources

3. Violence help hotlines | womenshealth.gov

https://www.womenshealth.gov/.../violence-help-hotlines.html

A project of the U.S. Department of Health and Human Services Office on **Women's Health**. Skip Navigation. ... **Violence help hotlines**. ... The **National** Domestic ...

4. Shop for NATIONAL HOTLINES FOR WOMEN

bing.com/images/shop

Abused Men: The Hidden Side of D...

Ovarian Cancer, Cancer Awareness…

5. Domestic Violence - National Hotlines & Resources …

feminist.org/911/crisis.html

National Hotlines. **National Domestic Violence Hotline** … **National** Battered **Women's** Law Project 275 7th Avenue, Suite 1206 New York, NY 10001 Phone: 212-741-9480

6. The National Domestic Violence Hotline | Contact

www.the**hotline**.org/contact

Media Contact. Each time a **domestic violence** story is covered, media has an opportunity to save lives. The **National Domestic Violence Hotline** is a leading …

7. National Hotlines and Helpful Links

www.victimsofcrime.org/…/national-hotlines-and-helpful-links

National Hotlines and Helpful Links. Victim Connect **National Hotline** for Crime Victims 1-855-4-VICTIM … **National** Indigenous **Women's** Resource Center 406-477-3896.

BY Publishing

ABOUT BY PUBLISHING & RHONDA BRANCH YEARBY

Rhonda Branch Yearby is a #1 International bestselling author, A successful grant writer, fundraiser, corporate/ religious event planner, songstress, & backup singer, President & CEO of Rhonda Branch Ministries. And founder of Women of Faith, Grant Seekers and BY Publishing projects of Rhonda Branch Ministries, talk show host of Keeping It REAL with Rev. Rhonda, ordained minister of the gospel, mother of 3 adult children, grandmother, great grandmother and happily married to her best friend Monroe M. Yearby, Jr.

BY Publishing's mission is to give author's a strong Christian voice and platform to teach, speak and preach to the world. **We sincerely believe that you do not have to break the piggy bank to share your story with the world and become a bestselling author!**

We provide a five-star signature, very inexpensive publishing, marketing, public relations and promotion service, we effectively assist authors to successfully publish and promote their life's works and truly connect to their friends, family and fans! We have a streamline system to launch you to a bestselling author.

45171726R00163

Made in the USA
San Bernardino, CA
02 February 2017